PHIL BRENNAN, KEITH DORRICOTT AND DON
WILLIAMSON

The Believer's Position and the Disciple's Practice

A Bible Study of the Book of Ephesians

First edition

This book was professionally typeset on Reedsy.
Find out more at reedsy.com

Contents

I

A Bible Study of Ephesians

This part of the book comprises thirteen modules, each containing the relevant passage of scripture, an introductory commentary and a series of questions for individual or group study.

Module 1: An Introduction to Ephesians

P aul, an apostle of Jesus Christ by the will of God, To the saints who are in Ephesus, and faithful in Christ Jesus: Grace to you and peace from God our Father and the Lord Jesus Christ. (Ephesians 1:1,2)

* * *

Ephesians is a clear presentation of foundational Christian truths – basic Christianity. It is a comprehensive, clear, practical and beautiful presentation of who we are; how we came to be what we are, what we shall be, and how we should live now in the light of that destiny.

The epistle outlines:

- what God has done *for* us and what God expects *from* us
- Christian *privilege* and Christian *responsibility*
- the *position* of the believer and the *practice* of the disciple
- the *doctrine* of faith and the *practice* of faith

The first set deals with matters of doctrine, theology and privilege, and is found in chapters 1–3. The second set deals with matters of practice and responsibility, and is found in chapters 4–6.

Ephesus

Located at the mouth of the Cayster River, on the east side of the Aegean Sea, the city of Ephesus was an important city on the west coast of Asia Minor (modern Turkey). Ephesus was the capitol of proconsular Asia and as such was the political and commercial centre of a large and prosperous region. Its port was large and provided a link between Rome and the East. Merchants flocked to it, Jew and Gentile mingled in its streets. It was a melting pot of nations and ethnic groups not unlike the character of Venice in the Middle Ages. In its day, Ephesus ranked with Alexandria in Egypt, and Antioch of Pisidia.

Ephesus boasted of its temple to Diana or Artemis (one of the Seven Wonders of the ancient world), and also of a theatre capable of holding an estimated 25,000 spectators. This was where citizens chanted "great is Artemis of the Ephesians" (Acts 19:29-40). To such a city, Paul came to preach. In such a place, God was pleased to establish a faithful church.

Evangelising and teaching in Ephesus

Paul visited Ephesus on his second missionary journey (Acts 18:19). Leaving Aquila and Priscilla there to carry on a work (Acts 19:24-26) that would see a church of God established (1 Corinthians 16:19).

Paul revisited Ephesus on his third journey (Acts 19), this time staying for perhaps three years (Acts 20:31) and leaving Timothy there for a further year and a half to continue the work, countering the false teaching of influential men such as Hymenaenus and Alexander (1 Timothy 3:20). There is a touching passage in Acts 20:17-38 telling of Paul's meeting at Miletus with the elders of Ephesus, as he made his way back to Jerusalem in time for Pentecost.

Paul's letter to the Ephesians

It appears most likely that Paul wrote his letter to the church of God in Ephesus while under house arrest in Rome (Acts 28:16-31) sometime between A.D.60-62 and the letter is therefore known as one of the "prison epistles" (along with Philippians, Colossians, and Philemon). Probably, the letter was carried by Tychicus along with the letter to the Colossians (Ephesians 6:21; Colossians 4:7). Thirty years or so later, the Lord Jesus gave to the Apostle John a letter for this church indicating its people had left their first love for Him (Revelation 2:1-7).

As already mentioned, the letter divides into two main parts: the first is doctrinal – the position of the Christian (1:1–3:21); the second is practical – the practice of the Christian (4:1–6:24). The first half of Ephesians lists the believer's heavenly possessions: adoption, redemption, inheritance, power, life, grace, citizenship, and the love of Christ. There are no imperatives in chapters 1-3. But in chapters 4-6 there are thirty-five directives that speak of the disciple's responsibilities to conduct himself according to his calling.

Opening salutation

Paul, an apostle of Christ Jesus by the will of God - an apostle was one appointed and sent by the Lord to be a recipient and authenticator of the New Testament revelation. This underlines the authority of what he was about to write. Then he says, *by the will of God*, removing the focus on himself as the messenger and pointing to divine sovereignty as the source of his work. There is no egotism with Paul. Rather, he sees himself as the recipient of divine grace. God had called him. God had also called the Ephesians to whom he wrote – not to apostleship but nevertheless, they were called of God.

To the saints who are in Ephesus ... faithful in Christ Jesus - there is no definite article before *faithful*, thus indicating that the *saints* and those who are *faithful* are one and the same.

Notice how believers are:

Saints – set apart to a special, sacred use in divine service. In this connection, see John 17:16-19; 1 Corinthians 1:30; 2 Thessalonians 2:13. Sanctification is first and principally a work of God. Then, people made holy and set apart by God are to show vigilance in maintaining their holiness by carefully observing the word of God (1 Thessalonians 4:3-8). Paul is about to remind the Ephesians of their position of holiness, given by God, and then go on to impress upon them their responsibility in maintaining holiness in life. Those whom God has made saints are called upon to be saintly.

faithful - this means firstly that they had exercised faith. They were believers. There is a beautiful expression of the working of faith in the case of Thomas given in John 20. Thomas' exercise of faith in the resurrection of the Lord Jesus went beyond an intellectual acceptance of the fact; it also touched his heart, and when that happened, he responded with commitment, declaring, "My Lord and my God." A second meaning of faithful is that those thus described continue in faith. They persevere, enduring to the end. Many believers refer to the doctrine of perseverance as referring to the perseverance of God in continuing faithfulness to us, enabling us to endure. Whilst that is true, it calls for those to whom God is faithful, to be faithful also. The Ephesians were displaying this character of the true Christian.

in Christ - We will come to this again under the modules 'The Position of the Christian,' but we note it here as the last of three things Paul said about those to whom he wrote. This is the first of nine such phrases in chapter one alone. Altogether, Paul uses the phrase "in Christ" or "in Him" 164 times in his writings. The phrase means more than believing in Christ. It means being joined to Christ in one spiritual body so that what is true of Him is true also of us. This truly is a stupendous truth.

> *"Union with Christ has its source in the election of God the Father before*
> *the foundation of the world and it has its fruition in the glorification of*

the sons of God. The perspective of God's people is not narrow; it has the expanse of eternity. Its orbit has two foci, one the electing love of God the Father in the counsels of eternity, the other glorification with Christ in the manifestation of His glory. The former has no beginning, the latter has no end."[1]

Grace to you and peace from God our Father and the Lord Jesus Christ - this may be a common greeting but how meaningful it is! The Ephesians lived in a world that was crassly commercial and materialistic. So do we. They lived in a city preoccupied with pagan practice involving sex and superstition. The cities we live in today are the same. What keeps disciples faithful to God in such environments? What enables us to live saintly lives? The answer is in the greeting. Our strength is in God's grace and it is there that we find real peace.

---

[1]   John Murray, *Redemption Accomplished and Applied*, Grand Rapids, Eerdmans, 1955

Module 1 Discussion Questions

1. What does the fact of the gospel reaching Ephesus tell us? (See Mark 6:5,11)
2. Looking at Acts chapters 18, 19 and 20, what strikes you most interesting about the work done in Ephesus? How might it apply today?
3. Discuss the cause and effect relationship of doctrine and practice. How important is teaching and why?
4. Of all the ways Paul might have introduced himself, he chose, "an apostle of Christ Jesus, by the will of God." What is the significance of these words?
5. Discuss the three elements of Paul's description of the Ephesians, taking note of how it makes you feel about the work of God in your life and how you are reflecting these attributes: (i) Saints (ii) Faithful (iii) In Christ.
6. In some ways Ephesus was a microcosm of the world we live in today. How does Paul's greeting to the church help you to face such a world?

Module 2: Chosen, Redeemed and Sealed

B lessed be the God and Father of our Lord Jesus Christ, who has blessed us with every spiritual blessing in the heavenly places in Christ, just as He chose us in Him before the foundation of the world, that we should be holy and without blame before Him in love, having predestined us to adoption as sons by Jesus Christ to Himself, according to the good pleasure of His will, to the praise of the glory of His grace, by which He made us accepted in the Beloved.

In Him we have redemption through His blood, the forgiveness of sins, according to the riches of His grace which He made to abound toward us in all wisdom and prudence, having made known to us the mystery of His will, according to His good pleasure which He purposed in Himself, that in the dispensation of the fullness of the times He might gather together in one all things in Christ, both which are in heaven and which are on earth—in Him. In Him also we have obtained an inheritance, being predestined according to the purpose of Him who works all things according to the counsel of His will, that we who first trusted in Christ should be to the praise of His glory.

In Him you also trusted, after you heard the word of truth, the gospel of your salvation; in whom also, having believed, you were sealed with the Holy Spirit of promise, who is the guarantee of our inheritance until the redemption of the purchased possession, to the praise of His glory. (Ephesians 1:3-14)

* * *

James Montgomery Boice wrote that "doctrine, if it is rightly understood, leads to doxology. If we discover who God is and what He has done for us, we will praise Him."[2] In Paul's mind, doxology was never far from doctrine. We often detect him singing in his epistles. That is what we have here. Verses 3 to 14 are all one sentence. Although often broken into several sentences in English translations, Paul begins with a note of praise to God for "every spiritual blessing," then keeps going, piling phrase upon phrase, doctrine upon doctrine. Gift after gift, wonder after wonder, is brought into view.

It has been called "a magnificent gateway" to the epistle, "a golden chain of many links," "a kaleidoscope of dazzling lights and shifting colours," and "a vast display of interconnected doctrines." It is not surprising that these verses form one sentence. It is like one mountain range of glorious, majestic peaks. Phrase is built upon phrase; glorious truth is added to glorious truth.

There is a Trinitarian structure to these verses: God the Father (vv.3-6); the Lord Jesus (vv.7-10); the Holy Spirit (vv.11-14). Our blessing comes from God the Father, becomes ours though the Lord Jesus, and are applied by the Holy Spirit. John Stott divided the paragraph as (vv.4-6) past blessing of election; (vv.5-8) present blessing of adoption; (vv.9-10) future blessing of unification, followed by a section on the scope of these blessings.[3]

Some of the content of the blessings referred to in verse 3 is enumerated in the verses that follow. There is:

the blessing of election (v.4) - we have been chosen by God so that we may be what we could never be by our own choice – "holy and without blame." Divine election makes it possible for us to make right choices (see Psalm 25:12). The spiritual blessings in the heavenly places in Christ cannot be obtained through

---

[2]   James Montgomery Boice, *Ephesians*, Baker Book House Company, 1997

[3]   John R.W. Stott, *God's New Society - The Message of Ephesians,* Downers Grove, Ill., Intervarsity, 1979

force, nor can they be earned, nor even obtained by request. Satan attempted to posses spiritual blessings by force. He tried to conquer heaven but failed, being himself conquered.

We cannot earn spiritual blessings. We don't possess the right currency. In our natural state, we are not the kind of persons who, unaided by God, will even ask Him for blessings. On the contrary, we despise His blessings. We want our own will and our own way and, left to ourselves, we would never ask God for anything. The only way these blessings may be received is as a result of God's own sovereign act, election. The blessings of salvation come to us simply because God has determined from before the foundation of the world to give them to us.

the blessing of adoption (v.5) – under Roman law, an adopted son had all the rights of a legitimate son. He was fully included in his new family and lost all rights to his previous family. In the eyes of the law he had become a new person, so that all debts and obligations were cancelled as if they never existed. Our adoption wipes out the past and assures us of a completely new life.

the blessing of redemption (v.7) – we have been bought out of slavery. We were in the grip of something that we were helpless to release ourselves from, having no power to redeem ourselves or to become free of the grip of sin.

the blessing of forgiveness (v.7) – the 'slate has been wiped clean.' To a sinner convicted of his sin there is no sweeter note in all the gospel than this. Forgiveness means that his sins have been lifted up from off him – thoroughly removed. Forgiveness comes through confession and repentance and once it is truly known, the relief is indescribable: it is the relieving of a burden we had no means of removing.

the blessing of revelation (v.9) – without this we could never properly understand history or make sense of life. The struggles of the broken world are not to go on forever. We have hope.

the blessing of sealing (v.13) - like an authenticated document and a possession marked for its owner, we are authenticated and marked as belonging
to God. The Holy Spirit is the guarantee (Gk. arrabon) – the deposit paid as
guarantee that more will follow.

the blessing of inheritance (vv.11,14) - we have an inheritance incorruptible,
undefiled, that does not fade and which is reserved in heaven for us (1 Peter
1:4). Not only do we have an inheritance but we are Christ's inheritance – "the
purchased possession."

> *He and I in that bright glory*
> *One deep joy shall share –*
> *Mine to be forever with Him,*
> *His that I am there.*
> (Mrs Bevan)

to the praise of His glory - three times in one sentence Paul uses this phrase. It
comes after the work of God the Father, the work of God the Son, and the work
of God the Holy Spirit. The glory of God is the ultimate and supreme purpose
of redemption.

Module 2 Discussion Questions

1. Thinking about how doxology follows doctrine, how does it make you think about Doctrine (teaching) and Doxology (e.g. hymn singing)? Can you think of particular hymns which you have found helpful in reinforcing teaching?

2. Imagine someone asks you, "If you believe God works all things according to the counsel of His will (Ephesians 1:11), and that His knowledge of all things past, present, and future is infallible, then what is the point of praying that anything happen or not happen?" How would you answer?

3. What are the 'spiritual blessings' referred to in this passage, and what does it mean that they are "in Christ"?

4. Do you think that perhaps 'physical blessings' are easier to keep in our minds and appreciate on a daily basis? How do we better appreciate the things God has given us that are mentioned in this passage?

5. What do you think the inheritance is that the Holy Spirit is a deposit of?

6. Paul speaks of a future redemption - but haven't we already been redeemed?

7. How does the repeated phrase, "to the praise of His glory" affect your thinking?

Module 3: Prayer for Revelation

T herefore I also, after I heard of your faith in the Lord Jesus and your love for all the saints, do not cease to give thanks for you, making mention of you in my prayers: that the God of our Lord Jesus Christ, the Father of glory, may give to you the spirit of wisdom and revelation in the knowledge of Him, the eyes of your understanding being enlightened; that you may know what is the hope of His calling, what are the riches of the glory of His inheritance in the saints, and what is the exceeding greatness of His power toward us who believe, according to the working of His mighty power which He worked in Christ when He raised Him from the dead and seated Him at His right hand in the heavenly places, far above all principality and power and might and dominion, and every name that is named, not only in this age but also in that which is to come. And He put all things under His feet, and gave Him to be head over all things to the church, which is His body, the fullness of Him who fills all in all. (Ephesians 1:15-23)

* * *

In the first half of the chapter, in one long sentence running from verse 3 to verse 14, Paul has been praising God for salvation of which He is both the author and accomplisher. God the Father chose; God the Son redeemed; God the Spirit applied that salvation in a personal way. But then, in the second half of the chapter, we have a prayer. The gist of this prayer is that God, who planned and accomplished salvation, might complete it as His people grow in knowledge of Him.

There is a deal of difference between knowing *about* God and knowing God. Paul was not praying that the Ephesians should grow in knowledge about God anymore than the Lord Jesus desired that we should only know about God. He said, "This is eternal life: that they may know You, the only true God, and Jesus Christ, whom You have sent" (John 17:3). Paul wrote to Timothy, "I know whom I have believed and am persuaded that He is able to keep that which I have committed to Him until that Day" (2 Timothy 1:12). In his book, *Knowing God*, J.I. Packer suggests the following three elements:

> *"First, knowing God is a matter of personal dealing ... It is a matter of dealing with Him as He opens up to you, and being dealt with by Him as He takes knowledge of you ... Second, knowing God is a matter of personal involvement, in mind, will and feeling ... The believer rejoices when his God is honoured and vindicated, and feels the acutest distress when he sees God flouted ... Equally, the Christian feels shame and grief when convicted of having failed his Lord ... Third, knowing God is a matter of grace. It is a relationship in which the initiative throughout is with God – as it must be, since God is so completely above us and we have so completely forfeited all claim on His favour by our sins."* [4]

Then Paul prays that they might, in their increasing knowledge of God, know also the key elements of the salvation that He has achieved for us. These are given here as:

the hope of His calling - God has called us to something and for something. It is very definite - we have not been called into a vacuum. The Bible does not use the word "hope" as it is commonly used in the world as referring to something uncertain and ill-defined. Neither is our hope only to be found in a future in heaven – there are aspects to it that are for the here and now. To be "holy and without blame before Him in love" (Ephesians 1:4); to be adopted "as sons by Jesus Christ to Himself" (Ephesians 1:5); to be for "the praise of

---

[4] J.I. Packer, *Knowing God*, Downers Grove, Ill. Intervarsity Press, 1973

the glory of His grace" (Ephesians 1:6). All this and more is included in the hope of His calling.

the riches of the glory of His inheritance in the saints - when God had redeemed Israel from slavery, he constituted them His People, and told them, "you shall be a special treasure to Me above all people; for all the earth is Mine. And you shall be to Me a kingdom of priests and a holy nation" (Exodus 19:5,6). Clearly such things matter a great deal to God and He highly treasures them. Paul's prayer was that the Ephesians should share that perspective.

the exceeding greatness of His power - the power here described is "the mighty power which He worked in Christ when He raised Him from the dead and seated Him at His right hand in the heavenly places." All the power of Satan must have been mustered against that work of God. To keep Christ dead and prevent His exaltation must have been their greatest goal. But God raised and exalted Him! Nothing could prevent that! And that same power is available to us!

How do you get to know a person – really know them? You must spent time with them. The degree to which the answer to Paul's prayer will be realised will be in direct relation to the time we spend in the presence of God in Bible study, in prayer and meditation. In his commentary on Ephesians, James Montgomery Boice tells the following story concerning Harry Ironside:

> *"Harry Ironside tells of meeting a very godly man early in his ministry. The man was dying of tuberculosis, and Ironside had gone to visit him. His name was Andrew Fraser. He could barely speak above a whisper. His lungs were almost gone. Yet he said, "Young man, you are trying to preach Christ, are you not?"*
>
> *"Yes, I am" replied Ironside.*
>
> *"Well," he said, "sit down a little and let us talk about the Word of God." He opened his Bible, and until his strength was gone he opened up one passage after another, teaching truths that Ironside at that time*

had never seen or appreciated. Before long tears were running down Ironside's cheeks, and he asked, "Where did you get these things? Can you tell me where I can find a book that will open them up to me? Did you get them in seminary or college?"

Fraser replied, "My dear young man, I learned these things on my knees on the mud floor of a little sod cottage in the north of Ireland. There with my open Bible before me, I used to kneel for hours at a time and ask the Spirit of God to reveal Christ to my soul and to open the Word to my heart, and he taught me more on my knees on that mud floor than I ever could have learned in all the seminaries or colleges in the world." 5

When Paul thinks about the power that raised Christ from the dead, he cannot help but find his mind expand to consider the glories of the Lord Jesus Christ. He "fills all things" for life apart from Christ is meaningless. This preeminent picture of our risen and exalted Saviour ought to affect us in two ways. First, it draws us to worship before One so exalted that He is over all things. If these closing verses still form part of Paul's prayer, then it is that we should be the more aware of the exaltation and the supremacy of Christ. Secondly, we should be astonished at what God has done for us in Christ. By union with Him who has been given to the church the Body as its Head, we are sharers in His glory.

Finally, note that Paul does not pray here that the Ephesian saints and, by extension, we, should be given this power of which he has been speaking; but that we might be aware of the power we already possess in Christ.

---

5   H.A. Ironside, *In the Heavenlies: Practical Expository Addresses on the Epistle to the Ephesians* Neptune, N.J., Loizeaux Brothers, 1937

Module 3 Discussion Questions

1. This is a letter addressed to a group of believers who are rich beyond measure in Jesus Christ. But is it possible for believers to live as spiritual paupers? What does spiritual poverty look like? What is the solution for it?

2. Why do you think Paul mentions "love for all the saints" (v.15)?

3. Paul prayed for the Ephesian saints. How important is it to pray for one another? And what exactly was it that Paul was praying for here? Discuss the difference between knowing about God, and knowing God.

4. What is your understanding of (i) the hope of His calling (ii) the riches of the glory of His inheritance in the saints and (iii) the exceeding greatness of His power?

5. If God has put 'all things under his feet,' explain 1 Corinthians 15:24-25. Does Hebrews 2:8 help?

6. What does this statement in verse 22 mean: "head over all things to the church, which is His body"?

7. What does "the fullness of Him who fills all things" (v.23), refer to and mean?

Module 4: Position of the Christian (1)

A nd you He made alive, who were dead in trespasses and sins, in which you once walked according to the course of this world, according to the prince of the power of the air, the spirit who now works in the sons of disobedience, among whom also we all once conducted ourselves in the lusts of our flesh, fulfilling the desires of the flesh and of the mind, and were by nature children of wrath, just as the others. But God, who is rich in mercy, because of His great love with which He loved us, even when we were dead in trespasses, made us alive together with Christ (by grace you have been saved), and raised us up together, and made us sit together in the heavenly places in Christ Jesus, that in the ages to come He might show the exceeding riches of His grace in His kindness toward us in Christ Jesus. For by grace you have been saved through faith, and that not of yourselves; it is the gift of God, not of works, lest anyone should boast. For we are His workmanship, created in Christ Jesus for good works, which God prepared beforehand that we should walk in them. (Ephesians 2:1-10)

* * *

Ephesians 1 takes us to a very high place but as we begin chapter 2, we find we have dropped off the cliff! Nostalgia rates fairly high in human interest. The BBC recently ran a TV series, "The way we were." That's what we have here in this chapter – without the nostalgia! It's a look back to the way we were.

The condition of human nature may be assessed in a variety of ways:

THE BELIEVER'S POSITION AND THE DISCIPLE'S PRACTICE

1. Basically OK. It is "well" as opposed to "sick." There may be admittance it is not as healthy as it ought to be, but there is no cause for alarm. History traces the evolution of human endeavour and things are getting better. At the worst, it is not quite perfect.
2. It is not well. In fact it is quite sick. There is certainly something wrong – but all is not hopeless. People are at least alive, and while there is life there is hope.
3. The state of human nature is absolutely hopeless. It is so serious that the only way of describing it is that it has gone beyond being sick, to being dead.

We are not free to please God. This has been debated at great length. Augustine, Luther, Calvin, Edwards – each had his own way of expressing it but all were agreed that apart from divine "quickening" (giving life), no-one ever turns to God to embrace salvation. That is what lies behind the starkly stated in the third condition in the list above - no other view does justice to what the Bible teaches concerning the nature of sin and the totality of grace in salvation.

Then notice that the "death" here spoken of is a strange death – for, although it has no ability to respond to God in righteousness, it is nevertheless active (*"walking," "conducted," "fulfilling desires")*. Sin leaves a permanent mark on our consciousness. Sin kills innocence. Sin kills ideals. Sin kills the ability to exercise the will. And, as if that were not bad enough, sin makes us the objects of God's wrath. If sin is to taken seriously then the wrath of God must also be taken seriously.

But God ... - God's intervention met all our need. For lost innocence – guilt was removed; for murdered ideals – lives were changed to be made able to achieve ideals again; for a destroyed will – we were given the ability to make right choices. And it gets better and better! In verse 5 and 6 most English versions have "together" three times; "made us alive together," "raised us up together," "made us sit together." We have already noted Paul's references in chapter 1 to the making alive, the raising up and the sitting down of Christ.

Here in chapter he speaks of what has happened to believers in Christ as a result of their union with Him in God's great work of salvation.

Verses 4-7 tell us of God's mercy, love, grace and kindness. We ought to spend time contemplating each part of this four-fold divine movement toward fallen humanity.

The richness of His mercy - mercy has the sense of favour being shown to those who deserve the precise opposite. The fact that we have not been the recipients of God's wrath is because God is merciful. It is not that we were simply helpless and lost and therefore deserved pity; we stood condemned. He reached out and saved us. Children of wrath have become objects of divine mercy! We have been saved not by merit but by mercy. Matthew Henry said, "All the compassions of all the tender fathers in the world compared with the tender mercies of our God would be but a candle to the sun or a drop to the ocean."

The greatness of His love - we are not able to measure nor comprehend the greatness of God's love. Scripture tells us of the greatest display of man's love, so it not surprising that we often go to the Cross to contemplate the greatest love of all. Of this, C S Lewis wrote:

> "God, who needs nothing, loves into existence wholly superfluous creations in order that He may love and perfect them. He creates the universe, already foreseeing – or should we say 'seeing'? there are no tenses with God – the buzzing cloud of flies about the cross, the flayed back pressed against the uneven stake, the nails driven through the mesial nerves, the repeated torture of back and arms as it is time after time, for breath's sake, hitched up ... Herein is love. This is the diagram of Love Himself, the inventor of all loves." [6]

The exceeding riches of His grace - grace means there is no cause in us why

---

[6]   C.S. Lewis, *The Four Loves*, New York: Harcourt, Brace and Co., 1960

God should have acted the way He did. We live in an age of "rights." We think we are owed certain things by reason of the kind of beings that we are. Many people even employ that sort of reasoning to their relationship to God. They expect God to act as if He owes us something. When He fails to do what they expect, they say, "It just isn't fair." So long as anyone thinks that way, they do not understand grace. Grace is God's favour to the utterly undeserving.

Someone has worked out an acrostic for grace as:

- Gift – the principle of grace
- Redemption – the purpose of grace
- Access – the privilege of grace
- Character – the product of grace
- Eternal Life – the prospect of grace

His kindness toward us in Christ Jesus - kindness might appear to be somewhat weaker than grace, love and mercy, but in fact it is not. It flows from God and there is no weakness in God. Somebody has said that kindness is the truest revealer of a person's greatness. There was a time in Elijah's life when it looked like it was all over. Read 1 Kings 19 for the details and you'll find the kindness of God shown in a remarkable way. The supply of rest, food and water, then the communication in the "sound of gentle stillness," and the restoration to service with a clear directive; this is how the kindness of God was shown to Elijah.

> *"Years ago I remember seeing the news report of a coal mining accident in the Allegheny mountains. Many minors escaped with their lives, but three men were still trapped somewhere deep within the earth's crust. Whether they were dead or alive, no one knew. What made the accident even more threatening to life was the presence of intense heat and noxious gases within the mine itself. If the men were not crushed by the rock, they could well have been asphyxiated by the fumes or killed by the heat. Two days went by before a search expedition was aloowed*

to even enter the mine because of the heat and fumes. Even then, there was great danger in store for anyone who would dare descend into what could well be a deep, black grave.

I don't remember what happened to those three men. All I remember is a brief interview conducted with one of the members of the search party as he was preparing to enter the mine. A reporter asked him if he knew of the noxious gases and the extreme danger of the mine. The man said, "Yes."

"Are you still going down?"

And the man said, "Those men may still be alive." Without another word of explanation, he put on his gas mask, climbed into the elevator, and descended into the black inferno of the mine." [7]

Ultimately, all illustrations of kindness fail before the greatest expression of all: "... But when the kindness and the love of God our Saviour toward men appeared ..." (Titus 3:4). We can only marvel at the realisation that God is not only sovereign, holy, and full of wrath against sin, but that he is also love, mercy, grace, and kindness, and praise Him for it.

Ephesians 2:8-9 is one of the best known passages of the Bible, and probably one of the most widely memorised texts. The text has three parts. The first tell us how God saves us, - "by grace"; the second, of the channel through which this grace of God comes to us – "through faith"; and the third, of how God does not save us – "not of works, lest anyone should boast."

Saved by grace - Paul insists that it is by grace we have been saved. We have not earned salvation nor could we have earned it. It is the gift of God and our part is simply to accept it. C.H. Spurgeon wrote:

"Because God is gracious, therefore sinful men are forgiven, converted,

---

[7] James S. Hewett, *Illustrations Unlimited*, Tyndale House Publishers

purified and saved. It is not because of anything in them, or that ever can be in them, that they are saved; but because of the boundless love, goodness, pity, compassion, mercy and grace of God."[8]

That's good because it not only defines "grace" but also points to what grace achieves. And that is the context in which grace is used here. We'll come to that when we look at verse 10.

Through faith - there are several misconceptions as to what faith really is. Faith is not a subjective feeling. It is not based upon a person's individual attitudes and feelings. Therefore it is not mere credulity. Neither is that form of optimism commonly referred to as "positive thinking." Norman Vincent Peale popularised this last view of faith with his book, *The Power of Positive Thinking*, in which he deals with several New Testament passages referring to faith. John Stott, who analysed Peale's view, says, "To Dr. Peale faith is really another word for self-confidence."[9] Faith, in the context of any of these human definitions is unstable and liable to disappoint. True faith is utterly reliable for it is faith in the trustworthy God, who never fails.

In the Biblical sense, faith has three elements. Spurgeon lists these as (i) knowledge, (ii) belief and (iii) trust. J. Montgomery Boice has them as (i) knowledge, (ii) heart response, and (iii) commitment. The exercise of faith then begins with knowledge of the gospel; and understanding of certain facts concerning ourselves, the condition we are in, and what God has done about it. John Calvin wrote:

"We shall possess a right definition of faith if we call it a firm and certain knowledge of God's benevolence toward us, founded upon the truth of the freely given promise in Christ, both revealed to our minds and sealed

---

[8] C.H. Spurgeon, *All of Grace*, Chicago, Moody Press

[9] John Stott, *Your Mind Matters*, Downers Grove Ill., Intervarsity Press, 1972

upon our hearts through the Holy Spirit."[10]

But faith is more than an intellectual assent to certain truths. It also involves a response to such knowledge. Therefore, Calvin also says:

> *"It now remains to pour into the heart what the mind has absorbed. For the Word of God is not received by faith if it flits about in the top of the brain, but when it takes root in the depth of the heart that it may be an invincible defence to withstand and drive off all the stratagems of temptation."*[10]

The final element is trust or commitment. It involves casting yourself upon Christ, resting on His promises, and accepting His finished work on your behalf. It is saying, as Thomas did, "My Lord and my God!"

Not of works – that must mean that faith is not a work. Nothing we can do, however great or small, can procure salvation. Salvation is by grace alone, through faith alone. Grace saves us – faith is the channel through which it flows. But then we reach verse 10. Whilst it is true that we are saved through faith alone, it is also true, as the old Reformers were fond of saying, that we are not saved through a faith that is alone. Faith leads us to good works.

The importance of a right understanding of these verses cannot be over-emphasised. The difference between Roman Catholic theology and Reformed theology is starkly evident in their understanding of these verses. Roman theology says: "faith plus works equals justification." Reformed theology says, "faith equals justification plus works" In other words, although works form no part of the procurement of justification, they are the necessary and inevitable proof of it. This is that element of God's salvation that Paul refers to in verse 5 where he tells us that God made us, who were spiritually dead,

---

[10] John Calvin, *Institutes of the Christian Religion*, ed. John T. McNeill, trans. Ford Lewis Battles. Philadelphia, Westminster Press, 1960

alive. That regenerating power not only provides eternal life but energises every aspect of Christian living. Augustine says that before we knew that regenerated life, we were, *non posse non peccare* ("not able not to sin"), but that by the new birth that joins us to the Lord Jesus Christ, we are now *posse non peccare (able not to sin),* and hence able to do good works. Before, we were utterly incapable of doing any good thing that could satisfy God, but now, as a result of the work of God, we are able to do truly good works.

Module 4 Discussion Questions

1. What does this passage teach concerning the condition of human nature, and what does it mean?
2. Discuss the following and make a note of particular points: (i) The richness of God's mercy (ii) The greatness of His love (iii) The exceeding riches of His grace (iv) His kindness toward us in Christ Jesus.
3. The word 'together' appears three times in the passage – what is the significance of that?
4. In what way are these three "together' things true of us when we are still on earth?
5. What does the thought of "sitting together in the heavenly places" convey to you?
6. What does it mean to be "saved by grace" "through faith" (provide definitions of "grace" and "faith")?
7. What is the relationship between good works and salvation?

Module 5: Position of the Christian (2)

herefore remember that you, once Gentiles in the flesh—who are called Uncircumcision by what is called the Circumcision made in the flesh by hands— that at that time you were without Christ, being aliens from the commonwealth of Israel and strangers from the covenants of promise, having no hope and without God in the world. But now in Christ Jesus you who once were far off have been brought near by the blood of Christ. For He Himself is our peace, who has made both one, and has broken down the middle wall of separation, having abolished in His flesh the enmity, that is, the law of commandments contained in ordinances, so as to create in Himself one new man from the two, thus making peace, and that He might reconcile them both to God in one body through the cross, thereby putting to death the enmity.

And He came and preached peace to you who were afar off and to those who were near. For through Him we both have access by one Spirit to the Father. Now, therefore, you are no longer strangers and foreigners, but fellow citizens with the saints and members of the household of God, having been built on the foundation of the apostles and prophets, Jesus Christ Himself being the chief cornerstone, in whom the whole building, being fitted together, grows into a holy temple in the Lord, in whom you also are being built together for a dwelling place of God in the Spirit. (Ephesians 2:11-22)

* * *

Verses 11 to 22 of chapter two repeats the pattern observed in the early part of the chapter where there is first a look back to what we were, and then a section on what God has done about our lost condition. In the first part of the chapter this method of teaching has to do with the individual; here, in the verses before us, it has to do with people together. There is a wrong way of "looking back" - as Lot's wife (Genesis 19:17, 26; Luke 17:32); But there is also a good and useful way (see Isaiah 51:1).

There are three parts to this present passage - What we *were* (our past); what we *are* (our present and future); there then follows a remarkable section beginning with the household of God and culminating with the temple of God. In sublime reasoning, Paul describes the blessings of God's dealing with Jew and Gentile that surpasses the blessings of the Old Covenant. In setting out these surpassing blessings, Paul first describes the extremity of the case – the hopelessness of the Gentile before he makes the case for the work of grace that has brought about reconciliation and immense privilege.

What we were (Ephesians 2:11–13)

Uncircumcised - this was a derogatory term used by the Jews of all Gentile people. In the Jewish mind it suggested inferiority in every sense. To David, for example, it was simply unthinkable that a Philistine should bring reproach on the army of Israel (1 Samuel 17:26). It was the Gentiles who were outcasts, objects of derision and reproach.

Without Christ - the Gentiles had no Messiah, no Saviour or Deliverer and were therefore without divine purpose or destiny.

Aliens from the commonwealth of Israel - unlike the Jews, Gentiles did not have God as their supreme King.

Strangers to the covenant of promise - Gentiles were not able to partake of the covenant blessings that granted Israel a land, a kingdom, a priesthood. We were like foreigners in a land in which we had no rights.

Without hope - Gentiles had no hope because they had received no promises. Without hope, all is lost. If there is no hope, there is nothing.

Without God - although Gentiles had many gods, they were without the one true God because they didn't recognise Him (Romans 1:18-26). God is the source of every good thing (James 1:17). Therefore, to be without God is to be without everything that is good.

Far off - This was the overall effect; they knew no closeness to God, nor any of the benefits that result from such closeness. This is the final gasp of despair.

Paul then moves to:

What, by the grace of God, we are (Ephesians 2:13–18)

Brought near - He begins where he left off in the first list – we who were far off have been brought near. The offence of sin that brought about an uncrossable distance has been settled through the atoning work of Christ Jesus (2 Corinthians 5:18-21).

Possessors of peace - not just 'peace' but Christ Jesus Himself. He is our peace. Having made peace by the blood of His cross, no one and nothing is able to undo what has been done.

Wall of partition broken down - the temple in Jerusalem had several courts. There was the court of the Priests; that was the innermost, closest to the Temple itself. Then there was the court of Israel into which any Jewish male could enter. After that there was the court of the women for Jewish women. Josephus describes how, from this court one descended by five steps to a level area in which was erected a five foot high stone barricade that went around the Temple enclosure; then, after another level space there were fourteen more steps descending to the court of the Gentiles. The wall dividing Jew from Gentile bore inscriptions at intervals, declaring "No foreigner is to enter within the balustrade and embankment around the sanctuary. Whoever is caught will have himself to blame for his death which follows." Imagine then how vivid a picture this phrase presented to both Jew and Gentile of the change brought about by Christ.

Enmity abolished – Not only has the ancient enmity between Jew and Gentile been abolished, but the estrangement that exists between God and the unreconciled sinner has also been settled.

Created as one new man – the Greek word for "new" here is *kainos*, indicating something that is qualitatively new. Gentiles were not made Jews, nor Jews, Gentiles. What Christ has done is to produce an entirely new person. Chrysostom said that it is as if one should melt down a statue of silver and a statue of lead, and the two should come out gold.

Reconciled to God – opposing things had not merely been made to settle their differences but, due to the new creation, there is harmony, peace, concord. But this goes further than the animosity that existed between Jew and Gentile; they have been reconciled to God. D. Martyn Lloyd-Jones in his extensive treatment of this passage says that the word reconciliation has five parts:

- First, it means a change from a hostile to a friendly relationship.
- Second, it means more than a mere settling of hostilities – as in formally estranged parties being on speaking terms again. Rather, it means really bringing together again, a reuniting, a re-connecting.
- Third, it is a word which emphasises an action that is complete. The enmity is so completely set aside that amity really exists. It is not a 'patch up.' It is not a compromise.
- Fourth, it is a word that implies that one of the two parties took the initiative. *Kata* indicates an action that comes down from above. It is

31

not that the two sides come together voluntarily; it is the one bringing the other into this position of complete amity and accord.

- And finally, in the fifth place, the word carries the meaning that it is a restoration of something that was there before.[11]

Having access to God the Father by the Holy Spirit - what liberty, what boldness we have in our approach to the Father! It is by Christ and through the Holy Spirit. What more could have been done? The Greek word here for 'access' is *prosagoge*. It is a word used of bringing a sacrifice to God; of bringing a person in before God that they may be consecrated; of bringing a speaker or an ambassador into a national assembly; and, above all, of bringing a person into the presence of a king. We have access to the throne room of God, to bring our troubles, sorrows, loneliness, to speak for others, and to offer ourselves, and to offer sacrifices of praise.

A glorious conclusion (Ephesians 2:19–22)

In this final section of chapter two there is a beautiful description of what divine grace has wrought – persons from all nations brought together, reconciled to God, beneficiaries of the peace made by the Lord Jesus through the blood of His cross, brought near as children to the Father, with access by the Spirit – this is all beautifully described as "the household of God" (v.19).

The phrase "the household of God" is variously understood to be a description of a building i.e. house, or a group or persons i.e. household. (Gr. oikeios = belonging to a house must be understood according to context, and some would reason that the context here points to a dwelling place rather than an aggregate of persons).

Either way, Paul is developing his argument that those reconciled "in one

---

[11] D. Martyn Lloyd-Jones, *God's Way of Reconciliation: Studies in Ephesians*. Grand Rapids, Baker, 1972

body," (best understood as a reference to the body of flesh of the Lord Jesus Christ rather than referring to the church the Body), have access to God by one Spirit; they have citizenship and sainthood; and they together with others similarly "framed", formed the temple of God, a habitation for God in the Spirit. It's important to remember that he was not writing to all the sects and divisions of the 21st century, but to people who were expressing obedience to the apostles' teaching and were thus aligned with the Chief Corner Stone.

It does seem likely that from the Roman prison, Paul's mind went back to that glorious edifice in Jerusalem – the temple. It was as if he was saying that what he saw in Ephesus was even more glorious. There were no longer divisions of courts, but, the way was open to all and, as one thing led to another, the final picture was of churches together forming one fellowship of churches called here a holy temple in the Lord ... a dwelling place of God in the Spirit. It was the grand ideal. It still is today!

The co-relation between the "Body" and the "Temple" has been variously understood and it's worth quoting at length here the comments of John Miller in his *Notes of the Epistles*, published by Hayes Press, originally in the Churches of God teaching magazine *Bible Studies*, and then in book form.

> "No doubt the reading of the King James Version has led many to conclude that the building mentioned here is the Church, the Body, but the correct rendering of the Revised Version "each several building," or the marginal rendering "every building" (Pasa Oikodome) shows that this cannot be so, for the Body which is composed of members is never spoken of as being comprised of buildings. What is here under consideration is not the Body of Christ but the Temple of God.
>
> Note how it is possible to destroy or corrupt the temple of God (1 Corinthians 3:16, 17); this could not be true of the Body of Christ. Each church of God is temple of God. Note the contrast between 1 Corinthians 3:16, 17 and 1 Corinthians 6:19; the former scripture is descriptive of the

church of God, while the latter relates to the believer's body. Thus we have:

1. *The believer's body is temple of the Holy Spirit (1 Corinthians 6:19);*
2. *The church of God is temple of God (1 Corinthians 3:16,17; 2 Corinthians 6:16); and*
3. *"each several building" (churches of God) fitly framed together, growth into a holy temple in the Lord (Ephesians 2:21).*

The last scripture views the temple as a whole. As illustrative of the buildings of the spiritual temple, note the action of the disciples with reference to the literal temple in Jerusalem: "His disciples came to Him to show Him the buildings of the temple" (Matthew 24:1). The temple was a pile of buildings joined together, built according to the mind of God. The words "fitly framed" are worthy of careful consideration as showing the intercommunion and fellowship which must exist between the several buildings, if there is to be such a thing in existence as "a holy temple in the Lord." Believers just meeting as Christians and each company a self-governing unit is foreign to the Scriptures."[12]

---

[12] John Miller, *Notes on Ephesians*, Hayes Press

Module 5 Discussion Questions

1. In what way is it right for us to look back – and in what ways are we not to look back?
2. Write a list of the things in verses 11–13 that we did not have, and then write over against them the things referred to in verses 13–18 that, by the grace of God we have. Looking over the two lists, how does it make you feel?
3. If Christ has 'abolished in His flesh the enmity, that is, the law of commandments contained in ordinances,' how do you explain Matthew 5:17?
4. What might the 'middle wall of separation' refer to?
5. How does the "reconciliation" and "peace" referred to here differ from the reconciliation and peace we often find in the world today?
6. What is your understanding of "the household of God"(v.19), and what do these verses tell us about it?

Module 6: Prayer for Realisation

For this reason I, Paul, the prisoner of Christ Jesus for you Gentiles— if indeed you have heard of the dispensation of the grace of God which was given to me for you, how that by revelation He made known to me the mystery (as I have briefly written already, by which, when you read, you may understand my knowledge in the mystery of Christ), which in other ages was not made known to the sons of men, as it has now been revealed by the Spirit to His holy apostles and prophets: that the Gentiles should be fellow heirs, of the same body, and partakers of His promise in Christ through the gospel, of which I became a minister according to the gift of the grace of God given to me by the effective working of His power.

To me, who am less than the least of all the saints, this grace was given, that I should preach among the Gentiles the unsearchable riches of Christ, and to make all see what is the fellowship of the mystery, which from the beginning of the ages has been hidden in God who created all things through Jesus Christ; to the intent that now the manifold wisdom of God might be made known by the church to the principalities and powers in the heavenly places, according to the eternal purpose which He accomplished in Christ Jesus our Lord, in whom we have boldness and access with confidence through faith in Him. Therefore I ask that you do not lose heart at my tribulations for you, which is your glory.

For this reason I bow my knees to the Father of our Lord Jesus Christ, from whom the whole family in heaven and earth is named, that He would grant you, according to the riches of His glory, to be strengthened with might through His Spirit in the *inner man, that Christ may dwell in your hearts through faith; that you, being rooted and grounded in love, may be able to comprehend with all the saints what is the width and length and depth and height— to know the love of Christ which passes knowledge; that you may be filled with all the fullness of God. Now to Him who is able to do exceedingly abundantly above all that we ask or think, according to the power that works in us, to Him be glory in the church by Christ Jesus to all generations, forever and ever. Amen.* (Ephesians 3:1-21)

* * *

In English idiom, "mystery" usually means something unknown and to be resolved by dint of human effort. To the Greeks of Paul's day it meant something known to the initiated. To Paul, it meant something unknown before the coming of Christ but which was now revealed; in particular, that Gentiles should be made partakers along with Jews of God's blessings concerning a people. That meant everything to Paul. It is why he broke off in verses 2 to 13 to speak about it. Here are a few of the thing that emerge from what he said. Such revelation of divine truth had given him:

A true evaluation of his imprisonment. Ultimately, he was not a prisoner of Nero or Rome, but of Jesus Christ. And it was for the sake of "you Gentiles" (the reason for his arrest that had led to his imprisonment). It was altogether a glorious and purposeful thing – he was not complaining!

A true evaluation of his ministry. He was the channel of life-giving water. The origin was God. The gospel was everything and to be marvelled at – not the messenger.

A true evaluation of himself. He was exercising the gift given him from God and any success in that was due to the "effective working of (God's) power."

A true evaluation of his suffering. To Paul, tribulation was an honour. He did not expect the way of salvation to be easy or trouble free. To suffer for Christ was not a penalty but an honour.

A true evaluation of history. From the constant struggle to bring meaning to chaos and to improve the world, Paul had come to realise that it was not after all about kings, queens, emperors, presidents, generals, inventors and scientists. The goal of human history was not ultimately about nations – their wars, battles and peace treaties - it was about the church.

Verses 14 to 19 concern another of Paul's prayers for the Ephesians. Notice his motivation – it was for them - that they should not become discouraged. Notice his resource – "according to the riches of (God's) glory" – it was inexhaustible. Notice its several specific requests:

that they should be strengthened with might through His Spirit in the inner man - spiritual power is a mark of every Christian who submits to God's word and Spirit. It is not reserved for some special class of Christian, but for all those who discipline their minds and spirits to study the word, understand it and live by it. Although the outer, physical person becomes weaker with age (2 Corinthians 4:16), the inner, spiritual person should grow stronger through the Holy Spirit's energising, revitalising and empowering.

that Christ should dwell in their hearts through faith - this cannot mean that there was a possibility of Christ not dwelling within – for then those Paul was addressing would have been unsaved. Every believer is indwelt by Christ at the moment of salvation (Romans 8:9; 1 Corinthians 12:13). Paul uses a Greek word here (katoikeo), which means to dwell in the sense of settling down, much as we would say, "to feel at home." He longs that the Ephesians should be in such a condition that Christ should be "at home." Such could only be the case where hearts are free from sin and lives are filled with the Spirit.

that they should be rooted and grounded in love - it is important for the growth of newly planted trees that they remain relatively motionless while their roots grow from the rootball into the surrounding soil. Root development includes the large structural roots along with the lateral growth of small absorbing roots. In time, a sufficient number of roots grow into the soil to anchor the tree. Excessive tree movement can hamper root development which, in turn, prevents the proper establishment of the tree. Paul prayed that the spiritual development of the Ephesians would not be hampered in any way, but that they should be rooted and grounded. Such stability and growth comes from being filled with self-giving, serving love for God and for His people (Matthew 22:37-39; 1 John 4:9-12, 19-21).

that they may be able to grasp the fullest dimensions of Christ's love - having prayed that love might fill and support them, he now prays that they might understand more of the source of such love. A full comprehension is impossible (v.19), but there are two ways in which we might "know" such love. What we cannot know exhaustively, we can nevertheless, know truly. That is to say, we ought to recognise true love by the love of Christ. Secondly, we are to increase in our awareness of His love. John Stott says of the four dimensions mentioned here, that:

> *"the love of Christ is broad enough to encompass all mankind (especially Jew and Gentile, the theme of these chapters), long enough to last fro eternity, deep enough to reach the most degraded sinner, and high enough to exalt him to heaven."*[13]

that they may be filled with all the fullness of God - the thought expressed here is perhaps the most stupendous of all.

> *"The phrase "fullness of God" can be either of two grammatical con- structions. It can be an objective genitive; in that case, the fullness of God would be the fullness of grace God bestows on us. Or it can be a substantive genitive; in that case, the fullness would be God's own*

---

[13] John Stott, *God's New Society: The Message of Ephesians*, Downers Grove,Ill., Intervarsity, 1979

fullness, that which fills Himself. Because if the preposition eis, which means, "unto," it seems that the second is to be preferred. Overwhelming as the petition may be, Paul seems to be praying that we (and all other Christians) may be filled up to or unto all the fullness that is in God Himself ... I think Paul is praying that we will be filled and filled and filled and filled – an so on forever, as God out of infinite resources increasingly pours Himself into those sinful but now redeemed creatures He has rescued through the work of Christ."[14]

To be so filled would mean there was nothing left of self. Though we cannot completely grasp the full extent of God's attributes and character – His power, majesty, wisdom, love, mercy, patience, kindness, and everything He is and does, we can, nevertheless, experience the greatness of God in our lives as a result of total devotion to Him. Even though Paul spoke this way, it is certain that he did not understand the full implication of his words. He has taken us to stand with him on the edge of infinity, gazing into the inexhaustible riches of God. Little wonder that he now breaks into one of his doxologies. Even though we will never comprehend the infinite, we may yet sense the substance of such things.

Even then, we feel like asking, "But how?" The theme is so high, surely it is unattainable! Paul points us to the One who is able. Our 'asking' seems too small a thing to bring in such grand result, but see what that asking is based upon. The structure rises like a mountain:

ask
all that we ask
all that we ask or think
above all that we ask or think
abundantly above all that we ask or think
exceedingly abundantly above all that we ask or think

---

14 J.M. Boice, *Ephesians,* Baker Book House Company, Grand Rapids, 1997

We have a God who is able to do things that we have not even dreamed of. Beyond all we have ever asked or thought, His ability lies unabated; His power is not diminished; and that power "works in us." Then Paul closes off the first section of his epistle with:

to Him be the glory in the church by Christ Jesus to all generations, forever and ever. Amen - when these marvellous requests are met and are enjoyed by faithful disciples, then God receives the glory and Christ is glorified with the honour He deserves from His people. The power is from Him – the glory must go to Him.

Module 6 Discussion Questions

1. Was Paul right to describe himself as 'less than the least of all the saints' - how should we view ourselves?
2. Considering the five noted points of Paul's evaluating, which of these helps you in your own evaluating of contemporary circumstances?
3. In what particular circumstances do you need to be "strengthened ... in the inner man"?
4. Why should Paul have prayed that "Christ may dwell in your hearts"?
5. What does it mean to be "rooted and grounded in love"?
6. What is your understanding of "the fullness of God"?
7. How does verse 20 make you feel about your prayers – the things we ask for? Will it change your attitude to prayer?

Module 7: Unity in the Church

I, *therefore, the prisoner of the Lord, beseech you to walk worthy of the calling with which you were called, with all lowliness and gentleness, with longsuffering, bearing with one another in love, endeavoring to keep the unity of the Spirit in the bond of peace. There is one body and one Spirit, just as you were called in one hope of your calling; one Lord, one faith, one baptism; one God and Father of all, who is above all, and through all, and in you all.* (Ephesians 4:1-6)

* * *

We have reached the point of transition from doctrine to duty, from principle to practice, from position to conduct. Precept ought always to precede practice. That is why "the apostles' doctrine" comes first in the list of four things that the church of God in Jerusalem continued steadfastly in. Without a good grasp of teaching, the community could never have come into existence, let alone be maintained. And how were they to engage in corporate worship and prayer, without that teaching? Doctrine and duty are never to be divorced. Teaching is not expendable; it is fundamental.

Paul exhorts them to "walk worthy of the calling with which you were called." Considering what we have read concerning our calling, that is a very high order! He has been dealing with such matters as predestination and election, adoption and redemption, the work of the Holy Spirit, rebirth, the work of God in reconciling people from all nations to Himself and to each other. As we have noted, the section then ends with a doxology. Yet Paul does not yet write 'finis' to his letter. To quote an old educational maxim, "input should equal output."

After the doctrine, there must be the application. We must strive for a balance in these things. Some might find it easier to concentrate on doctrine and know little of its practice. On the other hand, some are all about "doing" and find doctrine dry and impractical. Each of these is wrong. Doctrine without practice leads to dead orthodoxy; practice without doctrine leads to aberration.

walk - refers to daily conduct – manner of life.

worthy - means to have a worth equal to one's position. i.e. a "workman worthy of his hire" is one whose service merits the wages he receives. In our case, it is a manner of life that is commensurate with what God has done. This is not a matter of us choosing a vocation on the basis of our credentials. Remember, it is God who has chosen us, and He chose us with specific goals in view (Ephesians 1:4; Ephesians 2:10).

calling - it is God who has called; He has called us "out of darkness into His marvellous light" (1 Peter 2:9). We are no longer groping in the dark, therefore our conduct must reflect the fact that we can see.

with all lowliness and gentleness, with longsuffering, bearing with one another in love - later in this part of the epistle, Paul is going to write about specific relationships, but here is something that governs them all. This list of four cover-alls, involves not insisting on our rights but putting others needs before our own; not being self-assertive, but demonstrating the strength of meekness; not having a 'short fuse,' but showing real patience; and not reacting to the shortcomings of others, being willing rather to suffer wrong than to show retaliatory vengeance. These things are very different to the world culture in which we live. Disciples of the Lord Jesus are to demonstrate a life that is superior to the ungodly world and its ways.

44

the unity of the Spirit - it might be helpful to say what this is not. The unity of the Spirit is not uniformity. The manifestation of the gifts of the Spirit is seen in marvellous variety (1 Corinthians 12:4-6) that does not militate in any way against the thought of unity. In fact, that very diversity, blended together, is in itself a demonstration of what the unity of the Spirit really is. A piano would be a poor instrument if all the keys played the same note. Then, the unity of the Spirit cannot be achieved through ecumenicalism. For this unity to be "of the Spirit" means that it is brought about by His leading not our manoeuvring. It must therefore be in accord with Christ's teaching.

one body - the organic unity of a body is used as a metaphor for the church which consists of all believers since Pentecost until the Rapture. It's actually called the Church the Body of Christ (Ephesians 1:22,23; Ephesians 4:12-16; 1 Corinthians 12:12:27).

one Spirit - the Holy Spirit is the One through whom we were baptised into the one body. People come to a realisation of salvation through a variety of ways, but always through the working of the one Spirit (1 Corinthians 12:13).

one hope - 'hope' is used here in the way it is always used in scripture: to indicate something that lies in the future about which we have absolute certainty. This is important because the word 'hope' today usually infers a degree of uncertainty. Believers in Christ have a common hope that is sure and certain that they are all headed towards the day when there will be no divisions of race, experience, education or denomination; when they will be caught up together to be with the Lord Jesus for all eternity (Titus 2:13).

one Lord - refers to the Lord Jesus Christ, our Saviour. All believers have been made one in Him and are called upon to submit to His authority in obeying His commandments so that unity might be demonstrated by disciples on earth (Matthew 28:18-20).

one faith - this is best understood as a reference to the body of teaching that encompassed all that Christ taught His disciples (Jude 3). It was once for all delivered to the saints and therefore is not open to change with the winds of a thousand generations or cultures.

one baptism – there is no other means of identification with Christ.

one God and Father of all - opposed to the religions of the world, Christians believe in the Biblical emphatic teaching concerning the one true God (1 Corinthians 8:4). In Psalm 43, the psalmist says, "Oh, send out Your light and Your truth! Let them lead me; let them bring me to Your holy hill and to Your tabernacle. Then I will go to the altar of God, to God my exceeding joy" (Psalm 43:3,4). There is a progression there that gloriously culminates in enjoying the presence of God. Similarly, in our text of Ephesians 4:4-6 the work of the Spirit, the work of the Son, drawing us to the presence of the Father is seen in this seven-fold expression of divine unity. It ought to make us realise that the matter of Christian unity is extremely important as it ought to be a reflection of all that God is and has done.

Module 7 Discussion Questions

1. Chapter 4 begins a new section in the epistle. The first three chapters are concerned with doctrine; the second set of three chapters concerned with practice. In that context, discuss the principle of education, that input should equal output.
2. What is the meaning of the word "worthy" (v.1)?
3. Explain why (i) lowliness, (ii) gentleness and (iii) longsuffering are important attributes in the worthy life.
4. Does 'bearing with one another' simply mean putting up with people? Is it something your church needs to work on?
5. The Lord's prayer was "that they may be one" (John 17:21–23). Is this the same as "the unity of the Spirit"?
6. Make a list of the various instances of "unity" that are given in verse 2–6 and what strikes you about each.

Module 8: Purpose of the Gifts

B ut to each one of us grace was given according to the measure of Christ's gift. Therefore He says: "When He ascended on high, He led captivity captive, And gave gifts to men." (Now this, "He ascended"—what does it mean but that He also first descended into the lower parts of the earth? He who descended is also the One who ascended far above all the heavens, that He might fill all things.)

And He Himself gave some to be apostles, some prophets, some evangelists, and some pastors and teachers, for the equipping of the saints for the work of ministry, for the edifying of the body of Christ, till we all come to the unity of the faith and of the knowledge of the Son of God, to a perfect man, to the measure of the stature of the fullness of Christ; that we should no longer be children, tossed to and fro and carried about with every wind of doctrine, by the trickery of men, in the cunning craftiness of deceitful plotting, but, speaking the truth in love, may grow up in all things into Him who is the head—Christ— from whom the whole body, joined and knit together by what every joint supplies, according to the effective working by which every part does its share, causes growth of the body for the edifying of itself in love. (Ephesians 4:7-16)

* * *

The quotation from Psalm 68:18 is especially interesting. It takes us back to the triumphant bringing up of the Ark of the Covenant to Jerusalem in the reign of David (2 Samuel 6:12-19), and further back to the movement of the

Ark in the days of Moses (Numbers 10:35,36), the glorious fulfilment of which is seen here to be the ascending of the Lord Jesus in resurrection glory to His throne in heaven. In both cases there is the thought of God being exalted in the eyes of His people and of His response in sending blessing.

Viewed in relation to the ascension of the Lord Jesus, this response and the sending of gifts must be seen as essential to the continuing testimony of those Christ had redeemed. It was necessary that apostles, prophets, evangelists and pastor teachers were provided for the ongoing work of testifying to what Christ had done.

Verses 9 & 10 are properly in parenthesis. It is as if Paul can hardly help himself saying that if Christ ascended, it must mean that He first descended. There could have been no ascending from His eternal position as Son of God – there was nothing higher to ascend to. But He descended, "made Himself of no reputation, taking the form of a bondservant, and coming in the likeness of men. And being found in appearance as a man, He humbled Himself and became obedient to the point of death, even the death of the cross. Therefore, God also has highly exalted Him" (Philippians 2:7-9). The glorious result of His descending and ascending is that things that would otherwise have remained empty and void have been brought to fullness.

There are four principle passages where spiritual gifts are spoken of: Romans 12:3-8 Corinthians 12:1 -31, Ephesians 4:7–16, and 1 Peter 4:10,11. The reference in Ephesians (the one before us), is slightly different in that the "gifts" referred to are the "apostles ... prophets ... evangelists ... pastors and teachers." But the effect is the same. You have been given a spiritual gift to exercise for the glory of God and the good of others. That makes you a gift. You have been given a gift and you are given *as* a gift. That's what this passage is saying.

Of the four gifts mentioned there is a distinction between the first two and the last two. Apostles and prophets were given at the beginning of the church age because their ministry was foundational (Ephesians 2:20). Since the foundation has been laid, it is the responsibility of others to build on it and in accordance to its precepts and pattern. Evangelists and pastors and teachers are to do just that. They are not at liberty to change anything that the apostles and prophets received from the Lord in those early days and faithfully laid down for others to continue in.

An interesting change of emphasis is found in the insertion of a comma between "saints" and "for" in verse 12. If there is no comma, we understand that the work of these gifted men was to result in all the saints being equipped. The exercise of any individual gift ought to help another realise their gift and to exercise it. If, on the other hand, the insertion of the comma is correct, then the emphasis lies on the work of these gifted men being the work of "edifying ... the Body of Christ (etc.)." In any event, the result is the same, but it does seem important to point out that the work of edification (building up), is not the sole preserve of evangelists and pastors and teachers: it is something that we are involved in as we exercise the gifts that we have been given. Evangelists and pastors and teachers, building on the foundation laid by the apostles and prophets, help us to realise and to exercise our gifts so that others also are built up. his building up is described in seven stages of completeness:

till we all come to the unity of the faith - 'faith' here refers to the body of revealed truth that constitutes Christian teaching, the complete content of the gospel. The unity envisaged here is the oneness and harmony between believers made possible when it is built upon sound doctrine.

to the knowledge of the Son of God - the ever deepening knowledge of the Lord Jesus Christ through prayer, faithful study of His word and obedience to His commandments.

to a perfect man - this means, full grown, mature.

to the measure of the stature of the fullness of Christ - here is the standard:

Nothing less than the fullness of Christ. God's requirement of Abraham was so exacting; "Walk before me and be perfect" (Genesis 17:1). No less a goal is set before us.

no longer ... children - there is a difference between being childlike and being childish. Spiritual babes who never grow up are childish; milk feeders who should be on meat. We are not to be like that, "tossed to and fro and carried about with every wind of doctrine, by the trickery of men, in the cunning craftiness of deceitful plotting, but ..."

speaking the truth in love - it's possible to preach the truth and not have love; or to preach love and not have the truth. We need to get the mix right. Vance Havner used to speak about a man with one foot in hot water and one in ice-cold water, feeling very uncomfortable. But when he mixes the waters, he's quite all right. The truth will keep us from dissolving into sentimentality; love will keep us from hardening into severity.

grow up in all things into Him who is the head – Christ. We should grow out of childishness into childlikeness, learning things kept from the wise and prudent and revealed to babes, in simple faith learning obedience. The "all things" here envisages all-round development. There is no part of our lives that is exempt from this high ideal. We are to be completely yielded to Him, obedient to all that He has said, and Christlike in all areas of our lives.

Finally, we have a statement concerning the relationship of Christ to the Church which is His Body, and the outworking of that:

the Head - the authoritative leader. Paul wrote to the Colossians warning them of the possibility of "not holding fast the Head." When that happens, there can be no growth. Growth and nourishment for the Body (all the seven things listed in verses 13–15), come from union with the Head.

Module 8 Discussion Questions

1. What is the significance of the reference to Psalm 68:18 and of Paul's statement in parenthesis (vv.9,10)?
2. What is your understanding of verse 12?
3. Do you think verse 13 is a realistic goal here on earth?
4. How does the seven-fold list of verses 13–15 make you feel? What needs most attention? How can we better help one another towards this high goal?
5. What are the indicators that we, and those in our churches, are growing up (v.15), and working effectively (v.16)?
6. Is it easier to just 'speak in love' or to just 'speak the truth'? How about 'speaking the truth in love'? Can you think of some good scriptural examples?
7. What does "holding fast the head" mean in practice (Colossians 2:19) and what is its effect?

Module 9: Holiness in Life

This I say, therefore, and testify in the Lord, that you should no longer walk as the rest of the Gentiles walk, in the futility of their mind, having their understanding darkened, being alienated from the life of God, because of the ignorance that is in them, because of the blindness of their heart; who, being past feeling, have given themselves over to lewdness, to work all uncleanness with greediness. But you have not so learned Christ, if indeed you have heard Him and have been taught by Him, as the truth is in Jesus: that you put off, concerning your former conduct, the old man which grows corrupt according to the deceitful lusts, and be renewed in the spirit of your mind, and that you put on the new man which was created according to God, in true righteousness and holiness.

Therefore, putting away lying, "Let each one of you speak truth with his neighbor," for we are members of one another. "Be angry, and do not sin": do not let the sun go down on your wrath, nor give place to the devil. Let him who stole steal no longer, but rather let him labor, working with his hands what is good, that he may have something to give him who has need. Let no corrupt word proceed out of your mouth, but what is good for necessary edification, that it may impart grace to the hearers. (Ephesians 4:17-29)

* * *

What Paul says in verse 18 must have come as something of a shock to people living with the then Greek world-view. They regarded intellect as everything – the most noble and valuable, the best. Philosophy to them was a saviour.

53

Yet Paul speaks here of the futility of the unregenerate mind, a darkness in understanding, and alienation from the life of God. Note the culpability spoken of in verses 18 and 19. The wrath of God is revealed against ungodly people – not because they are innocently ignorant of Him, but because they wilfully set themselves against Him.

The one thing that really mattered is found in verses 20 and 21. The all-important issue? Learning Christ. No enlightenment can come from depraved minds. The only transforming power comes through the person and teaching of Jesus Christ; the only lasting changes take place in the life of the individual through believing in and learning from Him.

In 2007 the Prime Minister of Great Britain, Tony Blair said, "Ask me my three main priorities for government and I tell you *education*, *education*, and *education*." Blair's Minister of State for Education, Andrew Adonis, played a decisive role in turning this slogan into a reform programme for Britain's schools. When Paul speaks here of our spiritual schooling, he uses three Greek verbs. We might say that he was emphasising the importance of education, education, education.

The first word he uses is *emathete* and it is used to describe our learning as learning "Christ." It is more than learning the historical facts about a person; it means to learn a person. This is the same thought we were considering under Module 6: Prayer for Revelation (Ephesians 1:15-23) and linking John 17:3. It means that we have entered into a personal relationship with the living Lord Jesus Christ. It is a learning that changes us at the deepest level.

The second verb that Paul uses is *ekousate* and occurs in the phrase "you have heard Him." It is not that we have heard of Christ but rather that we have heard Him speak. Again, this is deeply personal. The way we hear the Lord Jesus Christ speak is through the Scriptures and as they are preached and explained to us. This had been the case for the Ephesians and it is true of us, too.

The third verb used by Paul is *edidachthete*. It is a heightened form of the common Greek word for instruction and occurs in the phrase, "(you) have been taught by Him." The preposition used in the NKJV here is poor. We would expect to read that we have been taught *by* the Lord, but the text is more accurately rendered, "(you) have been taught *in* Him." It suggests that the Lord Jesus is the school, as well as the teacher and the subject of instruction. He is the message, the means of our learning it, and He is the complete environment in which that learning takes place.

What is being emphasised here is the deep, profound and personal learning that takes place when believers truly exercise what is available to them. And it is a learning that leads somewhere. In verses 17 -19 Paul has been saying that the condition of depravity in the secular world is largely due to its wilful ignorance of God.

> *"The world has hardened its heart against God, and so is alienated from Him intellectually and in every other way ... The world is ignorant of God but Christians have come to know Him. The secular mind is hostile to Christ's teaching, the believer joyfully enrols in and continually makes progress in Christ's school."*[15]

We now come to a matter of putting off and putting on. To understand accurately what is being said here we must realise that this refers to something that has already been done. Paul is saying, "having learned, you were taught with regard to your former manner of life to put off the old self ..." The force of the argument is, "this being so – live like it!" It will necessarily involve:

Putting off lying – speaking the truth - *t*hat sounds straightforward enough, but there may be more to it than at first glance. In his first epistle, John refers to the spirit of antichrist (1 John 2:20-23) as *pseudo* ("the lie"). That is the same word Paul uses here. So firstly, the Ephesians are being reminded that

---

[15] J.M. Boice, *Ephesians,* Baker Book House Company, Grand Rapids, 1997

they have repudiated the lie and embraced the truth. Secondly, people who have embraced the truth should be truthful in word and conduct; they are to cultivate truthfulness.

> *"... if we are to grow as Christians, one of the necessary ingredients is cultivating truthfulness. We can lie quite deliberately, of course. A slander is a lie. A statement deliberately intended to mislead another person is a lie, particularly when the misleading is for our own advantage. But we can lie unintentionally just because we are not in the habit of rigorously cultivating truth."*[14]

Notice that Paul's reasoning on this point is that "we are all members of one another" (v.25). Earlier, he had spoken of the unity and health of the body being established through "speaking the truth in love" (v.15).

Putting off a wrong kind of anger – [by implication] be angry and sin not. Anger itself is not sin. There is unrighteous anger which is uncontrolled, and selfish, but there is also such a thing as righteous anger. Psalm 4:4, quoted by Paul here, makes a distinction between righteous and unrighteous anger. This is an important point: it is as wrong not to be angry in a situation demanding anger, such as gross injustice, as it is to be angry at the wrong time and for the wrong reasons. Again, the reasoning follows: anger must not be allowed to fester. This is particularly true of trouble arising between believers. If we can put the matter right, we must do so without delay. To allow it to swell and surge around like the tide gives the devil opportunity for making more trouble.

Putting off stealing – working - There are many different ways in which we can steal. It might seem incongruous to think of a Christian being guilty of petty or grand theft; but stealing has many masks. We steal from God when we set our own interests above those of God, or when we fail to worship Him as we ought, or when we waste time, talents, or resources that He has entrusted to us. We steal from our employer when we do not work to the best of our ability, or waste time, or leave work early. We can steal by overcharging, or by selling an inferior product, pretending it is better than it is. We steal by borrowing and not repaying. We steal by spoiling another's reputation.

It seems that Paul is chiefly drawing attention to the theft of not working or living in such a way that others have to take care of us when we are capable of taking care of ourselves. His direct word to such is, "do something useful with your hands." The reasoning section here is very interesting - Paul does not say that they should work in order to provide a better lifestyle for themselves, or to accumulate wealth for themselves. His argument is that by working hard they will be able to provide for those in genuine need.

Putting off corrupt talk – speaking to edify - the word translated "corrupt" also carries the thought of "corrupting," like the rotten apple that turns others rotten also. That is what some talk does. Christians must not be like that but be people whose words build up, whose speech is instructive, encouraging and uplifting. In this connection it's worth thinking about James' admonition in James 3:5,6. We ought to learn what good and what evil our speech can cause, and seek God's help in controlling our tongue. Frank E. Gaebelein wrote:

> *"Tongue control? It will never be achieved unless there is first of all heart and mind control ... When any Christian comes to the point of yielding to the Lord – in full sincerity, cost what it may – control of his thought life, the problem of managing his tongue will be solved, provided that such a surrender goes deeper than the intellect and reaches the emotions and will. For the Bible makes a distinction between mere intellectual knowledge of God and the trust of the heart."[16]*

It is at this point that Paul makes a comment which we might think could have been made in relation to many other things. He says, "And do not grieve

---

[16] Frank E. Gaebelein, *The Practical Epistle of James: Studies in Applied Christianity*, Great Neck, N.Y, Channel Press, 1955)

the Holy Spirit of God, (in) whom you were sealed for the day of redemption" (v.30). This teaches us that the Holy Spirit is a person who can be grieved. Many religious dogmas may teach us not to lie, to tell the truth, not to lose our temper but always to be controlled and disciplined, not to steal, not to use bad language or any sort of corrupt communication, to be good etc. – but here in this sublime communication from God, we learn that we are not to grieve the Holy Spirit.

And it is not only in the external things that are seen and heard by others; it is the attitude of heart and mind with which He is thoroughly cognisant; *anything that we may think or do that is not holy* grieves Him. He cannot leave us – we are sealed in Him for the day when unholiness will become an impossibility (see Romans 8:23). But in the meantime, our spiritual development, our growing up in all things into Him who is the Head – Christ, matters to Him. And so does our failure.

The section ends with verses 31 and 32 which are a kind of catch-all. Notice that six vices are met by 3 virtues. True goodness is always stronger than evil. "If you walk in My statutes and keep My commandments, and perform them ... you shall chase your enemies ... five of you shall chase a hundred, and a hundred of you shall put ten thousand to flight" (Leviticus 26:3,7,8). Bitterness, wrath, anger, clamour, evil speaking, and malice, are put to flight by kindness, tender-heartedness and a forgiving spirit.

Module 9 Discussion Questions

1. How would you describe your view of the world? Does it concur with that expressed by Paul in Ephesians 4:17-19?
2. How does your view of the world affect your behaviour?
3. What is the most important learning that can engage our minds, and how is it done?
4. What does it mean to 'impart grace to the hearer' and how do you do it successfully?
5. Working through the list of five specific examples of Christian conduct (vv.25–32), discuss each one, noting the negative (putting off), and the positive (putting on), giving examples of each. And note how these things affect the Holy Spirit. (i) Putting off lying – speaking the truth (ii) Putting off a wrong kind of anger – be angry and sin not (iii) Putting off stealing – working (iv) Putting off corrupt talk – speaking to edify (v) Putting off bitterness, wrath, anger, clamour, evil speaking and malice – being kind, tender-hearted and forgiving.

Module 10: Imitators of God

T herefore be imitators of God as dear children. And walk in love, as Christ also has loved us and given Himself for us, an offering and a sacrifice to God for a sweet-smelling aroma. But fornication and all uncleanness or covetousness, let it not even be named among you, as is fitting for saints; neither filthiness, nor foolish talking, nor coarse jesting, which are not fitting, but rather giving of thanks. For this you know, that no fornicator, unclean person, nor covetous man, who is an idolater, has any inheritance in the kingdom of Christ and God. Let no one deceive you with empty words, for because of these things the wrath of God comes upon the sons of disobedience. Therefore do not be partakers with them.

For you were once darkness, but now you are light in the Lord. Walk as children of light (for the fruit of the Spirit is in all goodness, righteousness, and truth), finding out what is acceptable to the Lord. And have no fellowship with the unfruitful works of darkness, but rather expose them. For it is shameful even to speak of those things which are done by them in secret. But all things that are exposed are made manifest by the light, for whatever makes manifest is light. Therefore He says: "Awake, you who sleep, Arise from the dead, And Christ will give you light."

See then that you walk circumspectly, not as fools but as wise, redeeming the time, because the days are evil. Therefore do not be unwise, but understand what the will of the Lord is. And do not be drunk with wine, in which is dissipation; but be filled with the Spirit, speaking to one another in psalms and hymns and spiritual songs, singing and making melody in your heart to the Lord, giving thanks always for all things to God the Father in the name of our Lord Jesus Christ, submitting to *one another in the fear of God.* (Ephesians 5:1–21)

* * *

Our last study in chapter 4 has been leading to this surprising statement in Ephesians 5:1 - "be imitators of God." The "therefore" links it with what has been said - transformation in Christ, and the empowering by the Holy Spirit – so that we might be imitators of God!

There are characteristics that belong uniquely to God, sometimes known as his incommunicable attributes: self-existence; self-sufficiency; eternality; omnipresence; omnipotence; omniscience. But then there are aspects of God's character that should be seen in us - sometimes called His communicable attributes: justice; wrath; wisdom; faithfulness; goodness; love; mercy; compassion; tenderness; forgiveness.

At first glance, "be imitators of God" seems to be an impossibly high ideal. It is reminiscent of the LORD's word to Abram in Genesis 17:1 "walk before me and be perfect." Yet, as we have seen, there is the transforming and the empowering. That is why this directive begins with "Therefore." We are without excuse.

> *"We are to imitate God "as dear children." In other words, just as a son should imitate a good father (though he is not a father and cannot imitate his father in many respects) and just as a daughter should imitate a good mother (though she is not a mother and cannot imitate her mother in many respects), so should the children of God imitate God."*[17]

Imbuing every aspect of that imitation of God, is love. Love that forgives and gives.

---

[17] J M Boice, *Ephesians,* Baker Book House Company, Grand Rapids, 1997

Love ever gives, forgives, outlives;
And stands with ever open hands:
And while it lives, it gives,
For this is love's prerogative
To give, and give, and give.

Love is unselfish in its giving. We are reminded here in verse 2 that Christ gave "Himself." Philippians 2:5-8 tells us that it was more than *things* that the Lord Jesus gave in order to save us. His outward glory, His position at the right hand of God the Father, the service of angels – these were accompaniments of His divinity - things of great and magnificent importance. He gave them up for our sake. But He gave more – He gave *Himself* to death on a cross. Greater love has no man than this. The greatest expression of love is not that it gives things or even that it gives up things, but that it gives itself.

The love that is spoken of here has been described as love that forgives, and gives and lives. We are to be ever ready to forgive, and ever willing to give. But our love is also to be reflective of God's eternal love – a living love; love that has the character of eternality about it; love that doesn't give up at the sight of opposition; that is not variable, faltering or untrustworthy. Solomon wrote, "Many waters cannot quench love, Nor can the floods drown it" (Song of Songs 8:7). When we read Romans 8:35-39, we realise how that has become real to us. God's love will never fail.

"Can you be an imitator of God in such an eternal love as that? The answer, if we look at ourselves, is no. No, we cannot. Nothing that is natural to us is eternal, or forgiving or giving either, for that matter. But the answer is yes, if we look to God. The very man who wrote Ephesians 5:1 said, "I can do everything through Him who gives me strength" (Philippians 4:13). But we must spend time with God for that to happen. The word that our text translates "imitate" or "imitator" is mimetai, *from which we get our English word "mimic." Mimic means to copy closely, to repeat another person's speech, actions, or behaviour.*

That is what we are to do with God. We are to repeat His actions, echo His speech, duplicate His behaviour. How can we do that if we do not spend time with Him? We cannot, because we will not even know what His behaviour is. Spend time with God! Spend time with God in prayer. Spend time with God in Bible study. Spend time with God in worship. It is only by spending time with God that we become like God. We need men and women who are like God today."[17]

Then in verse 3 and 4 Paul tells us that the disciple life must not bear even the hint of wickedness. It is to totally free of:

- *Sexual immorality* – the Greek word here is pornea and includes all sexual intimacy outside of marriage.
- *Impurity* – includes prostitution and homosexual practice.
- *Greed* – avarice, love of money; the intense aquisitional desire to have more.
- *Obscenity* – indecent action and words. No respect for standards.
- *Foolish talk* – to talk without intelligence. Making light of serious things
- *Course jesting.* Coarse, vulgar humour.

John Stott says of these last three, "All three refer to a dirty mind expressing itself in dirty conversation."

The expression, "but rather giving of thanks" may mean that to each of these prohibited activities, there is a corresponding activity of righteousness for which we should be thankful. Sexual union within marriage, material possessions to be unselfishly used, and an ability to speak true and valuable things.

Then follows the reason that such things must be far away from the Christian; they cause disinheritance in the kingdom of God, and they are a cause of God's wrath against unbelievers. The reasoning here is clear: Such practices belong to the world which is under, and yet shall face, the judgement of God. The believer has been saved from all that. He has been brought from darkness to light. What travesty then if the believer should appear to be the same as the darkened, lost soul who does not know God! Little wonder that such will lose their inheritance in the kingdom of God. Inheritance of the kingdom of God is based upon the subjection and obedience of the believer to the word of God. To forfeit such an inheritance is a serious matter.

The force of reasoning here is well described by John Stott:

> "Their theme (the theme of these chapters) is the integration of Christian experience (what we are), Christian theology (what we believe) and Christian ethics (how we behave). They emphasise that being, thought and action belong together and must never be separated. For what we are governs how we think, and how we think determines how we act. We are God's new society, a people who have put off the old life and put on the new; that is what He has made us. So we need to recall this by the daily renewal of our minds, remembering how we "learned Christ ... as the truth is in Jesus," and thinking Christianly about ourselves and our new status. Then we must actively cultivate a Christian life."[18]

Then we, who by God's grace are light, are to be an enlightening element in the darkness around us – God's light in the midst of this world's darkness. It is more than the fact that we have been transferred from the realm of darkness to the realm of light. Before, we were not only in darkness, but darkness was in us. Now, we are not only in the light but light is in us. The instruction of verses 15 and 16 is clear. We are to make the most of our time on this evil earth in fulfilling God's purposes, lining up every opportunity for worship and service. There is a wonderful thing said of David, that "after he had in his own generation, served the counsel of God, fell on sleep" (Acts 13:36 RV). David had an allotted time in which to serve God and he used it well.

---

[18] John R.W. Stott, *God's New Society: The Message of Ephesians*, Downers Grove Ill., Intervarsity Press, 1979)

We are to be "filled with the Spirit." This means that we should be so completely yielded to Christ that our thought and life are entirely taken up with Him and under the Holy Spirit's control. Evidence of being filled with the Spirit always manifests itself in obedience to the will of God and a faithful testimony to the Lord Jesus Christ.

The section closes with a reference to worship, praise and thanksgiving. When you look back over what we have been considering together, it's hard to imagine this was going to lead to anything else!

Module 10 Discussion Questions

1. Discuss the two options open to the believer – to imitate God or to imitate the world. Which is the easier, and why?
2. As 'children of the light' what difference should it make having Christians living in the world?
3. What are the 'unfruitful works of darkness' in today's world and how do we 'expose' them?
4. What do you understand by walking "circumspectly," and "redeeming the time" (vv.15,16)?
5. Are we really expected to sing 'to one another in psalms and hymns and spiritual songs'?
6. How do you, personally, try to make melody in your heart to the Lord?
7. What does being "filled with the Spirit" mean and how does it happen? How does it differ from baptism in the Spirit?

Module 11: Responsibilities at Home and at Work

Wives, submit to your own husbands, as to the Lord. For the husband is head of the wife, as also Christ is head of the church; and He is the Savior of the body. Therefore, just as the church is subject to Christ, so let the wives be to their own husbands in everything. Husbands, love your wives, just as Christ also loved the church and gave Himself for her, that He might sanctify and cleanse her with the washing of water by the word, that He might present her to Himself a glorious church, not having spot or wrinkle or any such thing, but that she should be holy and without blemish. So husbands ought to love their own wives as their own bodies; he who loves his wife loves himself. For no one ever hated his own flesh, but nourishes and cherishes it, just as the Lord does the church. For we are members of His body, of His flesh and of His bones. "For this reason a man shall leave his father and mother and be joined to his wife, and the two shall become one flesh." This is a great mystery, but I speak concerning Christ and the church. Nevertheless let each one of you in particular so love his own wife as himself, and let the wife see that she respects her husband.

Children, obey your parents in the Lord, for this is right. "Honor your father and mother," which is the first commandment with promise: "that it may be well with you and you may live long on the earth." And you, fathers, do not provoke your children to wrath, but bring them up in the training and admonition of the Lord. Bondservants, be obedient to those who are your masters according to the flesh, with fear and trembling, in sincerity of heart, as to Christ; not with eyeservice, *as men-pleasers, but as bondservants of Christ, doing the will of God from the heart, with goodwill doing service, as to the Lord, and not to men, knowing that whatever good anyone does, he will receive the same from the Lord, whether he is a slave or free. And you, masters, do the same things to them, giving up threatening, knowing that your own Master also is in heaven, and there is no partiality with Him.* (Ephesians 5:22-6:9)

* * *

Earlier, we pointed out that Ephesians is in two parts – doctrinal and practical. This is typical of Paul's writing; first the doctrine, then the application. We have now reached an interesting sub-division in this second part. The second half of the second half of the letter deals with relationships. The Christian's Spirit-filled life is not measured by his or her private morality alone, or even by their own private spiritual experience. It is also to be known in their relationship with other persons. The verses before us in this section deal with three sets of relationships: that of wives to husbands and husbands to wives; that of children to parents and parents to children, and that of slaves (servants, employees) to masters.

The relationship of marriage

It has often been pointed out that when Paul wrote this passage, he was "setting forth an ideal which shone with radiant purity in an immoral world." In Jewish, Greek and Roman society, the marriage bond was under severe threat. That is no less true of most cultures, in most countries today.

Not only is marriage a most precious relationship in life but it also reflects the relationship between Christ and the Church the Body. That puts the teaching of these verses at a very high level indeed. When, as is usual in the UK, the person officiating at a wedding says, "Marriage must not be entered into unadvisedly or lightly; but reverently, soberly and in the fear of God," it is with that high order of things in view.

It is impossible to speak too highly of the importance of marriage. It is the first human institution on earth, being the first relationship between human beings that God created. From this first institution that dealt with education, health care and rule, have sprung schools and universities, hospitals and clinics, and government. Marriage is under severe attack today. If it is allowed to decline, then the institutions that have developed from it will decline also. But it is even more serious than that. Walter A. Maier wrote:

> *"Because marriage comes from God above and not from man or beast below, it involves moral, not merely physical, problems. A sin against the commandment of purity is a sin against God, not merely the outraging of convention, the thoughtlessness of youth, the evidence of bad taste. The Saviour tells us that, when God's children are joined in wedlock, they are united by God, and beneath the evident strength and courage and love that this divine direction promises there is a penetrating, ominous warning. Those who tamper with God's institution have lighted the fuse to the explosive of retributive justice. Marriage is so holy that of all social sins its violation invokes the most appalling consequences ... Throughout history red blotches of warning mark the final record of devastated nations that forgot the divine origin of marriage and its holiness."*[19]

Relationship of wives to husbands

The basis of the marriage bond is love. Sometimes the word, "submit" (v.22) has led to an undue emphasis being placed on wives being subordinate to their husbands. No such emphasis is in the text. Rather, as we have said, the emphasis is clearly on love. The word, submit is qualified by "as to the Lord." Would any child of God respond to the Lord in the way too often portrayed as a brow-beaten, subservient menial? We love Him who first loved us – and our response to that is the willing, sweet submission of love.

---

[19] Walter A. Maier, *For Better, Not for Worse* St. Louis: Concordia 1935

Once that is settled, there ought to be no railing against the clear teaching of Scripture that a wife is to assume a subordinate role in the home. It is not a lack of equality, for all are made in the image of God and are equally valuable to God. Moreover, the subordination involved is voluntary. No woman need accept the proposal of any man. However, if she does voluntarily accept that proposal and enter into marriage, she thereby accepts the headship of her husband over her and promises submission to him. There may be thousands of women who rail against this and thousands of men who give them cause, but a Christian woman will nevertheless desire and seek to live up to God's standard.

It is worth pointing out that in the matter of the church being subject to Christ as Head, that it is not open to question. It is matter of divine decree and is eternally unalterable. The same applies then to the relationship of a wife to her husband. God has ordained an order of rule and men and women are called upon to recognise that and to behave accordingly. Refusal to do so will surely bring divine censure.

Relationship of husbands to wives

Nothing in the above statements give the husband the right to act as a petty tyrant. Nothing could be further from the instruction that he is to love his wife as Christ loves the church. It's not difficult to see how this whole thing works out. No woman would have a problem submitting to a husband who loves like that, who loves her enough to die for her.

Several things are said here about Christ and the church which, in context ought to instruct us in the matter of the relationship of husbands to wives. We are reminded that Christ "loved the church" (v.25). This is love of the highest standard; love that is completely unselfish; love that is sacrificial, for we learn that Christ "gave Himself up for her" (v.25). Next we read that Christ's goal was to "sanctify and cleanse her." So a husband's love is that which sets his wife apart from every other woman so that she can be to him what no other can. Then, his love must be a purifying love. Any "love" that drags a person down is false. Perhaps the greatest point in this is that a husband is to love his wife so as to encourage her spiritual development. John Stott says:

> *"a husband should never use his headship to crush or stifle his wife, or frustrate her from being herself. His love for her will lead him to an exactly opposite path. He will give himself up for her, in order that she may develop her full potential under God and so become more completely herself."*[20]

Relationship of children to parents

The fundamental relationship of children to parents is obedience. Children are to be willingly under the authority of their parents with obedient submission to them because that is the way that God has designed it. This means it is more than a matter of Christian ethics. It is recognised and taught by all the world's cultures, both ancient and contemporary. There is obligation not only on the child to obey, but also on the parent to enforce the obedience. Obedience to parents is one of the foundational things in God's will for mankind. However, the phrase, "in the Lord"(v.1), is probably best understood to refer to children being brought up in the environment of obedience to divine rule being manifest i.e. the kingdom of God.

In his book, God's New Society: The Message of Ephesians, John R.W. Stott points out that in the traditional Christian handling of the Ten Commandments the rule "Honour your father and your mother" (Exodus 20:12), the fifth of the ten, is placed in the second table of the law which deals with human relationships, while in the Jewish handling of the Ten Commandments it is placed in the first table, which deals with our relationship to God. Stott argues that the Jewish tradition is "surely right." It is because obedience to parents

---

[20] John R.W. Stott, *God's New Society: The Message of Ephesians,* Downers Grove Ill: Intervarsity Press 1979

is part of our relationship to God and because disobedience to parents is at heart a spiritual rebellion. Stott also points out that this is why under Jewish law the most extreme penalty, death, was proscribed for anyone who cursed his or her parents or was incorrigible in relationship to them. (cf. Leviticus 20:9; Deuteronomy 21:18-21).

Children are also to honour their parents. While obedience involves action, honour speaks of attitude – the motive behind the action. Paul points out that this is the first commandment with a promise. This does not mean that those who keep this commandment will necessarily live longer than any individual who does not, but that divine judgement in the taking of life may well take place on those who transgress this law. On the other hand, the law provided that very best way to live a long and happy life (Deuteronomy 5:33; 6:2; 8:3; 11:8,9). One of the characteristics of the "last days" is disobedience to parents (2 Timothy 3:1,2). Then, it can never be forgotten that it is recorded of the Lord Jesus that as a boy He went down to Nazareth, and He was subject to Joseph and to Mary (Luke 2:51).

Relationship of parents to children

We have already pointed out the duty of parents to ensure that their children obey them. Either part of this relationship makes demands on both parties. If children are to obey their parents, then parents ought to give them proper directions to obey; if children are to honour their parents, then parents ought to make sure they are worthy of that honour.

There are two parts to the instruction to parents, one negative and one positive. Parents are not to exasperate their children by unreasonable demands that drive to anger, despair and resentment (cf. Colossians 3:21). The positive part is to bring them up in the training and admonition of the Lord. This means of course, that patents will have to be well versed in the mind of the Lord. Again, the dual responsibility of parents and children is clear.

"Children, where God has graciously given such, are a sacred charge, and are to be brought up as God would have them and with the end in view that they may become useful in the Lord's service. Many lives are wasted in youth, as a tree may be spoiled in the early years of its growth. As truly as the body of the child needs great care when young, so truly does the mind. A spoiled child when grown up becomes wilful, selfish and proud. But where the discipline and admonitions of the Lord have been administered and the child in early years has been reproved and checked from going in the ways of folly and encouraged to tread the path of virtue, then we may expect plants and corner stones which go to the making of a happy people (Psalm 144 12-15).

Parents who smile at the folly of their children, and are pliable when they should be firm, are "making a stick to beat themselves with," and are doing their children irreparable damage. "Chasten they son, seeing there is hope; and set not thy heart on his destruction" (Proverbs 19:18 also see Proverbs 22:6).[21]

Relationship of slaves to masters

This is now the third actual example given of what was said by commandment in Ephesians 5:21: "Submitting to one another in the fear of God." We do well to treat this admonition as applying to employees and employers. In the first place, employees are to obey their employers. (As in the case of parents and children, this assumes that they are not instructed to disobey God.) Employers have the responsibility of making decisions of what should be done and how it is to be done. The responsibility of the employee is to obey their employer in these areas. The employee is to show respect and reverence – considering their employer's role as determined by God; with sincerity, loyalty and goodwill – not putting up a front, but willingly giving their best, putting their "heart and soul" into their work.

---

[21] John Miller, *Notes on the Epistles*, Hayes Press

Relationship of masters to slaves

As in the child/parent, parent/child relationship, each party has their re-
spective duty. By making the same application as above, (employees and
employers), here, the instruction is that there should be mutual honour and
respect from Christian employers to employees.

> *"The Spirit-filled boss uses his authority and power with justice and*
> *grace – never putting people under threats, never abusive or inconsider-*
> *ate. He realises that he has a heavenly Master who is impartial (cf. Acts*
> *10:34; Romans 2:11; James 2:9)"*[22]

---

[22] John MacArthur, *The MacArthur Study Bible*, Word Publishing, 1997

Module 11 Discussion Questions

1. How does a biblical view of marriage differ from that which is prevalent in our society? How can we seek to uphold it?
2. Discuss the qualifying statements made in respect of the wife's submission and the husband's love: "as to the Lord" and "as Christ also loved." Which partner do you think has the most difficult standard to live up to?
3. In this passage, what strikes you about the intimate relationship between the Church the Body and Christ?
4. What does it mean to 'admonish' your children?
5. What lessons can we learn about parenting from good and bad examples in the Bible?
6. Have you managed to obey the commands of vv.6-9 in a work environment? What would you say are the main challenges and keys to success?
7. What lessons can we learn about the servant/master relationship from good and bad examples in the Bible?

Module 12: Conduct in the Conflict

Finally, my brethren, be strong in the Lord and in the power of His might. Put on the whole armor of God, that you may be able to stand against the wiles of the devil. For we do not wrestle against flesh and blood, but against principalities, against powers, against the rulers of the darkness of this age, against spiritual hosts of wickedness in the heavenly places. Therefore take up the whole armor of God, that you may be able to withstand in the evil day, and having done all, to stand.

Stand therefore, having girded your waist with truth, having put on the breastplate of righteousness, and having shod your feet with the preparation of the gospel of peace; above all, taking the shield of faith with which you will be able to quench all the fiery darts of the wicked one. And take the helmet of salvation, and the sword of the Spirit, which is the word of God; praying always with all prayer and supplication in the Spirit, being watchful to this end with all perseverance and supplication for all the saints ... (Ephesians 6:10–18)

* * *

We are at war! Some people might say we are to think positively and peacefully; that the Christian life is not about entering into battle but exiting from it; that Christianity is about smooth paths and plain sailing. Scripture tells us that is not so. We are at war. This is not a viewpoint of pessimism and gloom; the final victory in the war is already settled and we are assured of many victories toward that final day.

Our adversary is opposed to God and all that is His so when we become God's children and seek to do His will, we are in Satan's firing line. But we need not fear – we are well equipped. These verses are not only a warning about the war but instructions on how to win. The adversary is extraordinarily powerful, but we have been issued with sufficient armour to combat and to thwart him. Sometimes we hear of armies whose soldiers have been issued with sub-standard equipment. That is not the case with the Christian engaged in spiritual warfare. We are the best-equipped foot soldiers the world has ever seen.

The warfare we are engaged in often has an effect in "flesh and blood" – but this warfare originates beyond the material and the physical. Though affecting the physical it is much more – it is essentially spiritual. This makes it the more serious and threatening. If the world's problems were merely material, they would have been fixed centuries ago. Clearly, man is not master of all – there are forces that are stronger than man, forces that stand behind the material world. It is all too easy to become lulled into a false sense of security – to let our guard down, thinking that the world we live in is not quite so bad after all. The reality is very different.

> *"This is a day of sorcery, demonic deception in the end of time. The world is tricked, fascinated, under the spell of a thousand evil eyes. The weird, the uncanny, the occult, psychedelic drugs, hallucinations – with these humanity is being swept into an orgy of induced insanity. The church is attacked, and Satan would deceive the very elect. Good men are led astray by the liberal gospel, the secular gospel, the social gospel. Jannes and Jambres imitate Moses. The great deceiver as an angel of light imitates every work of God, and thousands of poor souls cannot distinguish wheat from tares. Fortune-tellers, necromancers, magicians, are small fry compared to the new witchery let loose upon the world.*
>
> *Men we never dreamed would weaken are giving way, and Satan has so cleverly maneuvered his strategy that it appears un-Christian to lift a*

voice against his wiles and devices. This procedure is so skilfully executed,
that many are afraid to express even doubt of it – much less opposition.
We had better take some lessons in Ephesians six, and learn the true
nature of spiritual conflict. We have been provided full equipment for this
warfare, and we had better learn how to evaluate both our adversaries
and our allies."[23]

Notice the four times "against," in this passage, emphasising that we are really up against it!

1. *Rulers* – suggests regional influence, particular areas where demonic influence has been allowed to take a hold.
2. *Authorities* – effect perceived values – what is deemed acceptable, promoted or prohibited.
3. *Powers* – has to do with control.
4. *Spiritual forces of evil in heavenly places* – the forces against which we struggle are mighty and destructive.

The enemy may be extremely powerful but he is not omnipotent. It comes as a tremendous relief then to know that we are not called upon to face this formidable foe in our own strength.

The instruction to stand fast is "in the Lord." That not only implies obedience, but should also make us conscious of His authority. There is no greater authority than that.

Each piece of the armour is "the armour of God" (see Isaiah 59:17) - so it is God's truth, for example, not any truth.

The belt of truth: involves not only truthfulness but 'the truth' i.e. the body of teaching given by the Lord. For the soldier, his belt gathered in his tunic and

---

[23] Vance Havner, *The Vance Havner Notebook*, Baker Book House, Grand Rapids, Michigan, 1989

helped him in freedom of movement. We do not grope our way through life, guessing this and that; we move freely and quickly because we know the truth.

The breastplate of righteousness: involves not only righteousness imputed but also practiced. It has been said that when a man is clothed in righteousness, he is impregnable. A breastplate protected the heart and other vital organs. Practical, daily righteousness protects. A lack of personal holiness expressed in righteous assessment and deeds will leave us vulnerable in vital areas and may bring death.

Feet shod with the gospel of peace: indicates a readiness to tell others about the truth. Shoes carry us from place to place. If we are not properly shod, we will be immobilised – unable to take the gospel to others.

The shield of faith: may picture not only protection but (as in the Roman army) a means of moving forward in formation with others. The Roman soldier had two shields – one, a small round shield used in hand to hand combat, and the other a large oblong shield covering the soldier completely. It is the word for this larger shield that Paul uses here. It pictures soldiers advancing in rows, row upon row, shoulder to shoulder; the enemy faced with an impregnable solid wall of shields.

The helmet of salvation: includes the past, present and future aspects of salvation. It was said of the troops of Oliver Cromwell that they never lost because, being Calvinists, they knew that their destiny was secure and that they were fighting because God led them to that spot and would prosper them in that work. In a sense, the same is true of us. A true sense of salvation, past and future will help us realise our experience of present salvation. Paul wrote:

"We are hard-pressed on every side, yet not crushed; we are perplexed, but not in despair; persecuted but not forsaken; struck down but not destroyed ... therefore we do not lose heart ... we do not look at the things which are seen, but at the things which are not seen. For the things which

are seen are temporary, but the things which are not seen are eternal" (2 Corinthians 4:8,9,16,18).

The sword of the Spirit: the Greek word for "Word" here is 'Rhema' meaning "a word/saying." It indicates the day-by-day application of some part of the Word of God (as the Lord used it in the wilderness temptations).

Prayer: reminds us of our tremendous resource. We are never left alone in the struggle in a place where we cannot call for help. The fourfold use of "all" here is inclusive of various types of prayer, on all occasions, at all times, for all the saints.

Module 12 Discussion Questions

1. "The Christian life is a battleground, not a playground." How does that affect our attitude and behaviour?
2. We are commanded twice to put on the 'whole' armour of God - why is this so important?
3. We are also commanded to 'stand' - what does standing signify?
4. Discuss the following six items of armour, making a note of how each piece is useful: (i) the belt of truth (ii) the breastplate of righteousness (iii) feet shod with the preparation of the gospel of peace (iv) the shield of faith (v) the helmet of salvation (vi) the sword of the Spirit.
5. Hebrews 4:12 says the Word of God is sharper than any two-edged sword - useful in attack and defence - in what ways should we be careful not to mishandle it and cause damage?
6. What do the three 'alls' of Ephesians 6:8 tell us about how prayer should be deployed in spiritual warfare?

Module 13: Conclusion

... and for me, that utterance may be given to me, that I may open my mouth boldly to make known the mystery of the gospel, for which I am an ambassador in chains; that in it I may speak boldly, as I ought to speak. But that you also may know my affairs and how I am doing, Tychicus, a beloved brother and faithful minister in the Lord, will make all things known to you; whom I have sent to you for this very purpose, that you may know our affairs, and that he may comfort your hearts. Peace to the brethren, and love with faith, from God the Father and the Lord Jesus Christ. Grace be with all those who love our Lord Jesus Christ in sincerity. Amen.
(Ephesians 6:19-24)

* * *

A praying man knows the power of prayer and desires the prayers of others on his behalf. If Paul felt such a need, it stands to reason that all who seek to serve the Lord need the prayer support of others. Notice the particular request for prayer here. Paul does not ask for personal well being, or for comfort, nor even for release from prison. His only desire was that he might be granted boldness and faithfulness in proclaiming the gospel, no matter what the cost.

For Paul, specific prayer and effective witnessing went hand in hand. You and I might think that, of all people, the apostle Paul would not need the prayers of others to help him to speak fearlessly. You only need read the last eight chapters of the book of Acts and note the seven recorded occurrences of his speaking, to realise how this minister of the gospel used words powerfully and with boldness. Yet here, as he wrote his letter to the Ephesians, with all that experience behind him, he still yearned for the prayers of others that he might be given words and that he might be bold in expressing them. Sometimes we might be inclined not to pray for some people because we feel that they are good at what they do and therefore don't need our prayers. This request by Paul teaches us otherwise.

There's another detail in these closing verses regarding prayer. Paul says that Tychicus will let the Ephesian saints know Paul's affairs. Prayer warriors need to be informed of what they are praying for. That is not always possible, but where it is, we should seek to let others know of our specific needs and know theirs also.

The final benediction (vv.23,24) mentions peace, love with faith and grace. There are probably no greater treasures. These are four great words of the gospel, and for Paul that gospel continued to course through his being. The Gospel was not something to leave behind and move on, but a continuing dynamic with which to live. It lifts us above the humdrum and the horrible, the ordinary and the offensive.

Grace had begun the epistle; grace had been its subject; now grace concludes it. The spiritual blessings enumerated and taught ensured that Paul and all like him were not left to the confines of prison chains. The prisoner in Rome had greater riches than the emperor, greater power than the senate, and a peace that Rome never knew. Cyprian, a third-century martyr wrote long ago to a friend, Donatus:

> *"This is a cheerful world as I see it from my garden under the shadows of my vines. But if I were to ascend some high mountain and look out over the wide lands, you know very well what I should see: brigands on the highways, pirates on the sea, armies fighting, cities burning; in the amphitheatres men murdered to please applauding crowds; selfishness and cruelty and misery and despair under all roofs. It is a bad world,*

Donatus, an incredibly bad world. But I discovered in the midst of it a quiet and holy people who have learned a great secret. They are despised and persecuted, but they care not. They are masters of their souls. They have overcome the world. These people, Donatus, are the Christians – and I am one of them."

There is something marvellously unselfish about Paul's closing words to the Ephesians. When he does get to speak about his own condition, that too was for the sake of others. He did not complain about his chains nor deprivation, but he was concerned that they might be overly concerned for him. Self-sacrifice and consideration for others are the hallmark of the Christian.

"His imprisonment had not silenced him; his chain had not bound the fluency of his tongue, nor had his experience damped the fervour of his spirit. He would speak and speak boldly. But he was human and liable to depression and discouragement. He was a man of like passions with us. He needed to pray and be prayed for. He was Christ's ambassador whom the Lord had allowed to be bound, and though His servant and representative was bound He had not broken off negotiations with His enemies. Paul the servant and ambassador knew well his Master's mind and would yet plead with his enemies boldly to accept the terms of peace which were offered in the gospel.

He would wax more bold as grace was given him through the supplication of the saints, and he would boldly press the claims of his Divine Master on men. To settle down, to relax into quietness, would be fatal to the cause into which he had thrown himself heart and soul and for which was a prisoner of Rome. Rome had a mission, but he had a message. Theirs was to subdue nations and to rule the world with iron rule. But his was to give liberty, that men might come under the golden rule of his divine Sovereign."[24]

---

[24] John Miller, *Notes on Ephesians*, Hayes Press

So Tychicus would have carried, not only the letter to Ephesus and beyond, but also the news of Paul's condition, not of complaint, but of compassion for others; not of bemoaning his lot, but of blessing for others. They must have been encouraged!

Module 13 Discussion Questions

1. What is the difference between prayer and petition?
2. What is praying in the Spirit?
3. Why do we need to be alert when we are praying for other people?
4. In requesting prayer for himself, why did Paul not ask for prayer that he may be released from prison to avoid the hardship of it?
5. Have you ever prayed for an opportunity to faithfully tell the gospel? How did God answer?
6. Can you think of other scriptural examples of where God put someone in a difficult situation for a purpose? What about your own experience?
7. Paul closes his epistle by commending to them 'peace,' 'love,' and 'grace.' Are these just words – just a standard closing? What does he really want for them, and how could they have it?

II

Topical Studies in Ephesians

The Sovereignty of God in Ephesians

"He CHOSE us in Him before the foundation of the world, that we would be holy and blameless before Him. In love He PREDESTINED us to adoption as sons through Jesus Christ to Himself, according to the kind intention of His will, to the praise of the glory of His grace, which He freely bestowed on us in the Beloved." (Ephesians 1:4-6)

"having been PREDESTINED according to His purpose who works all things after the counsel of His will." (Ephesians 1:11)

"God, being rich in mercy, because of His great love with which He loved us, even when we were dead in our transgressions, MADE US ALIVE together with Christ (by grace you have been saved), and raised us up with Him, and SEATED US with Him in the heavenly places in Christ Jesus." (Ephesians 2:4-6)

* * *

One of the matters that the epistle to the Ephesians raises is God's sovereignty. For example, in Ephesians 1:5, 11, it refers to God predestining us: "In love He predestined us to adoption as sons through Jesus Christ to Himself, according to the kind intention of His will", and "In Him also we have obtained an inheritance, having been predestined according to His purpose who works all things after the counsel of His will."

The subject of God's sovereignty can be difficult for us to understand completely, as it can appear to conflict with our free will to believe or not for salvation. For example, the Scripture in Acts 13:48 ("When the Gentiles heard this, they were glad, and glorified the word of the Lord: and as many as were ordained to eternal life believed") can make it appear that it is entirely predetermined, which appears to conflict with Scriptures such as John 3:16 which says that: "Whoever believes in Him shall not perish, but have eternal life." It can seem to us unfair that people would be condemned to eternal judgment if they have no control over that decision. The apostle Paul wrote more than anyone else in Scripture about the sovereignty of God, especially in Romans chapter 9, and yet no one was more concerned about the need to preach the gospel to people that they might believe and be saved than he was. And so what can we learn about this important matter from Scripture?

God predetermines certain events, including the eternal salvation of certain individuals before they are born:

- "As many as were appointed to eternal life believed." (Acts 13:48)
- "We should always give thanks to God for you, brethren beloved by the Lord, because God has chosen you from the beginning for salvation through sanctification by the Spirit and faith in the truth." (2 Thessalonians 2:13)
- "God, who had set me apart even from my mother's womb and called me through His grace." (Galatians 1:15)

However this does not mean that the others who are doomed had no choice; it is based on the perfect foreknowledge of God:

- "They are without excuse. For even though they knew God, they did not honor Him as God or give thanks." (Romans 1:20,21)
- "Chosen according to the foreknowledge of God the Father." (1 Peter 1:1,2)
- "You do not believe because you are not of My sheep." (John 10:26)

God knows everything, and so He knows in advance who will respond to His

Word and believe it - "God is greater than our heart, and he knows everything" (1 John 3:20). Based on this foreknowledge, it seems that He predestines certain individuals to eternal life by them positively responding to His call in the gospel. He equips them to believe, to fulfill His appointment of them to eternal life. Then at some point in their lives He calls them in the gospel:

"Those whom he foreknew he also predestined [foreordained] to be conformed to the image of his Son, in order that he might be the firstborn among many brothers. And those whom he predestined he also called, and those whom he called he also justified, and those whom he justified he also glorified." (Romans 8:29-30)

Scripture makes clear that, in this period of time between Christ's return to heaven & His return to earth, "whoever believes" in Christ will be eternally saved; their faith is the key. ("Whoever wills" is, however, not a Scriptural expression in this context.) Similarly, in other dispensations of time, faith in what God has said is the key:

- "For God so loved the world, that he gave his only Son, that whoever believes in him should not perish but have eternal life." (John 3:16)
- "if you confess with your mouth Jesus as Lord, and believe in your heart that God raised Him from the dead, you will be saved." (Romans 10:9)
- "Everyone who calls on the name of the Lord will be saved" (Romans 10:13)
- "Jesus answered and said to them, 'This is the work of God, that you believe in Him whom He has sent.'" (John 6:29)
- "The Scripture has shut up everyone under sin, so that the promise by faith in Jesus Christ might be given to those who believe." (Galatians 3:22)
- "Without faith it is impossible to please Him, for he who comes to God must believe that He is and that He is a rewarder of those who seek Him." (Hebrews 11:6)

Many Old Testament examples are given of this - "All these, having gained approval through their faith, did not receive what was promised" (Hebrews 11:39)

Belief is a matter of personal choice, using faith in the revelation from God's Word; that faith is initially a gift from God:

- "For by grace you have been saved through faith. And this is not your own doing; it is the gift of God, not a result of works, so that no one may boast" (Ephesians 2:8-9)
- "Earnestly desire the greater gifts"... "now faith, hope, love, abide these three." (1 Corinthians 12:31; 13:13)
- For this reason they could not believe, for Isaiah said again, 'He has blinded their eyes and He hardened their heart, so that they would not see with their eyes and perceive with their heart, and be converted and I heal them.'" (John 12:39-40)

It would therefore seem that, based on the foreknowledge of God that they would not use the faith in God's Word if it were given to them, some people are not given during their lifetime sufficient faith to believe:

- "Each according to the measure of faith that God has assigned." (Romans 12:3)
- "According to the proportion of his faith." (Romans 12:6)
- "The devil comes and takes away the word from their heart, so that they will not believe and be saved." (Luke 8:12)
- "Not all have faith." (2 Thessalonians 3:2)

As a result, only those who are appointed to eternal life believe, and yet it is based on their response. This is completely fair, since none of us deserve it. All salvation is only by God's mercy:

- "There is no injustice with God"... "It does not depend on the man who wills or the man who runs, but on God who has mercy." (Romans 9:14,16)

- "The gifts and the calling of God are irrevocable." (Romans 11:29)

Salvation requires preaching in one form or other, which is generally how God calls people to Himself. Only some people positively respond to it by faith:

- "How are they to hear without someone preaching?" (Romans 10:14)
- "Whoever does not believe will be condemned." (Mark 16:15)

God may harden the hearts of those who continually refuse to believe His Word. This isn't due to any failure of the Word that they have received.

- "It was of the Lord to harden their hearts ... that they might receive no mercy." (Joshua 11:20)
- "It is not as though the word of God has failed." (Romans 9:6)

It requires that, as a believer, we exercise this faith given by God in prayer, to ask for things in Christ's name (which is more than just saying that in words). There appears to be some latitude within God's pre-determined will for believers today to receive, or not, certain of His blessings and answers to prayer based on their obedience by faith, within what He permits by His will:

- "If you ask Me anything in My name, I will do it." (John 14:14)
- "In everything by prayer and supplication with thanksgiving let your requests be made known to God. And the peace of God, which surpasses all comprehension, will guard your hearts and your minds in Christ Jesus." (Philippians 4:6-7)
- "Always in my prayers making request, if perhaps now at last by the will of God I may succeed in coming to you." (Romans 1:10)

The Lord's response to the disciples' question was (in Luke 17:6) "If you had faith like a mustard seed, you would say to this mulberry tree, be uprooted and be planted in the sea; and it would obey you." It might not be apparent what He was telling them, unless we go back to Luke 13:18,19 to something else He had told them about mustard seed: "He was saying, What is the kingdom of God like, and to what shall I compare it? It is like a mustard seed, which a man took and threw into his own garden; and it grew and became a tree, and the birds of the air nested in its branches." In other words, just as mustard seed has to be planted in order to grow, so our faith has to be applied for it to grow. And then it can become very large.

Back at the foundation of the world, when God predestined certain individuals to eternal life, making them His "elect" (just as He also has elect angels), He recorded their names in His "book of life," together with the inheritance He intended to give them.

- "Who will bring a charge against God's elect? God is the one who justifies." (Romans 8:33)
- "Those who dwell on the earth, whose name has not been written in the book of life from the foundation of the world, will wonder ..." (Revelation 17:8)
- "The rest of my fellow workers, whose names are in the book of life." (Philippians 4:3)
- "if anyone's name was not found written in the book of life, he was thrown into the lake of fire." (Revelation 20:15)

During this present "age of grace," no individual's name can be removed from this book, since the Holy Spirit has sealed them in their salvation eternally:

- "By grace you have been saved." (Ephesians 2:9)
- "We are not under law but under grace." (Romans 6:15)
- "God, who also sealed us and gave us the Spirit in our hearts as a pledge." (2 Corinthians 1:21-22)

In other ages, however, it was and will be possible through willful disobedience. In any dispensation, it seems that a person's inheritance blessings (in their lifetime and in the future) can subsequently be removed by God from the book of life due to serious disobedience:

- "May they be blotted out of the book of life and may they not be recorded with the righteous." (Psalm 69:28)
- "He who overcomes ... I will not erase his name from the book of life." (Revelation 3:5)
- "The unrighteous will not inherit the kingdom of God?" (1 Corinthians 6:9)

In every case, as a result of all this, everything unfolds according to the counsel of God's sovereign will, to His glory.

"To do whatever your hand and your plan had predestined to take place." (Acts 4:28)

The Glorious Gospel in Ephesians

For some people the word 'gospel' has become so associated with a six-thirty (or thereabouts) Sunday meeting, that it means little more than a public address often seemingly aimed inappropriately at the wrong audience. Many people assume that 'the gospel' is something we preach to unsaved people and that it is therefore irrelevant to those who are saved. Holding a 'Gospel Meeting' when the usual audience is made up of saved people, seems, to many, to be inappropriate.

Is such a view what Paul had in mind when he asked the Ephesians to pray for him, that **"utterance may be given to me, that I may open my mouth boldly to make known the mystery of the gospel"** (Ephesians 6:19)? Is this what it means to be **"fellow heirs, of the same body, and partakers of His promise in Christ through the gospel"** (Ephesians 3:6). In this section, we want to expand our appreciation of what the gospel actually is; to increase our sense of dependence on God in proclaiming it; to develop our skill in the handling of it, and to simply enjoy both the message of the gospel and the thought of sharing it with others.

> From the glory and the gladness, from His secret place;
> From the rapture of His presence, from the radiance of His face –
> Christ, the Son of God, hath sent me through the midnight lands;
> Mine the mighty ordination of the pierced hands.
> Mine the message grand and glorious, strange, unsealed surprise,
> That the goal is God's beloved, Christ in Paradise.

Hear me, weary men and women, sinners dead in sin;
I am come from heaven to tell you of the love within;
Not alone of God's great pathway leading up to heaven;
Not alone how you may enter stainless and forgiven –
Not alone of rest and gladness, tears and sighing fled –
Not alone of life eternal breathed into the dead –
But I tell you I have seen Him, God's beloved Son,
From His lips have heard the mystery He and His are one.

(Mrs. Bevan)

The following notes are taken from the minutes of an address given by Andy McIlree at the 2003 Churches of God Conference of Overseers:

When the One who said, "I am the Light of the world" also said, "you are the light of the world", He did two remarkable things: He showed that our humanity would be elevated to proclaim the focus of Deity and He conferred on His witnesses the greatest responsibility ever granted to servants of God. Isaiah's graphic picture of Him who "measured the waters in the hollow of His hands and measured out heaven with a span" (Isaiah 40:12) emphasises the sheer impossibility of our hands ever equalling His. How well He knew that our hands, so incapable of tracking the dimensions of the galaxies, would be equally incapable of tracing the doctrines of the gospel, yet He called us to handle the only message that can bring men and women to experience the eternal dimensions of the "new creation." The honour was equally expressed when Paul took Isaiah's words – "How beautiful are the feet of Him" (Isaiah 52:7) – and, by the Spirit, said, "How beautiful are the feet of them" (Romans 10:15).

The Kind of Preaching – the content of the message

1 Thessalonians 1:2-6 and 2:4 give a wonderful summary, covering the sower, the seed and the soil. Firstly, Paul, Sylvanus and Timothy's satisfaction is summed up in their thanking, mentioning, remembering and knowing, which

shows how conscious they were that the purpose of the gospel rests entirely on the sovereignty of God. Secondly, the produce of the gospel came from the good soil of believing hearts whose commitment was driven by the spiritual mainspring of faith, love, and hope. Thirdly, we are presented with the all-important aspect of God's pleasure in the gospel, so we are left in no doubt that the purpose of this glorious message is that it was designed to produce and to please.

The faithful sower can be faithful to the soil only if he is faithful to the seed. Perhaps, there are times when lack of production results not from trying to sow in the wrong soil but from attempting to sow with the wrong seed. Germinations depends on putting the right seed into the right soil, so each sower can stand between two works of God. If we don't depend on the inspiration of the seed there will be no germination in the soil.

When Paul said "our gospel did not come to you in word only" (1 Thessalonians 1:5), he raised the possibility of others preaching in an ineffective manner. His fear was "lest the cross of Christ be made of no effect" (1 Corinthians 1:17). Then he asked, "Do I now persuade men, or God? Or do I speak to please men? For if I still pleased men, I would not be a bondservant of Christ" (Galatians 1:10). This is the high price of inadequate content: it fails to make the hearer true to the cross, and it fails to keep the preacher true to Christ. People-pleasing and playing to the gallery are room-mates of what Job called "speaking unrighteously for God" (Job 13:7). Methods can undermine the message, therefore we need to follow Paul's approach: "in power" – with spiritual energy and impact; "in the Spirit" – He knows the Saviour best, He knows the sinner best, He knows and speaks the message best; "in much assurance" – preaching with knowledge and conviction, responding in the same way.

We must retain the grandeur of the message for misrepresenting God is a disservice to Him and to the sinner. For faith to have substance, we need to present a message with substance. Acts 17:2-4 shows that the wealth of

God's provision in sound gospel content lay at the foundation of the work in Thessalonica: reasoning ... explaining ... demonstrating ... persuading. Like regeneration, justification and redemption, crucifixion was a doctrine to Paul, not only an action. Before speaking to Galatia about a crucified Christ being clearly portrayed or placarded before them – he said, "I have been crucified with Christ" (Galatians 2:20; 3:1). Such was his expectation that the truths of the gospel would become living realities to those who believe.

Like him, we have the opportunity to confront man's ungodliness by presenting Christ, "the mystery of godliness" (1 Timothy 3:16). There can be no knowledge of salvation without knowing they are lost; no rescue without repentance; no pardon without guilt; no following the Saviour without forsaking sin; and no certainty of heaven without being faced with hell. It's unthinkable that anyone we know should never hear about hell because we don't love them enough to tell them! Sensitively, we can fulfil the kind of uncompromising preaching of which it was said that the preacher, "shook people over hell". Whether in public preaching or in private conversation, our aims are two-fold: to make them feel comfortable and uncomfortable, accepted and unacceptable. We are presenting a Person, not selling a product, therefore inviting lives that are ruined by ambition or addiction to "Try Jesus" is another gospel! We must emphasise the essentials and not be content with cosy homilies and anecdotal chats.

The Kind of Preacher – the character of the messenger

"What kind of men?" was vital too. Paul wanted people to sense God's appeal – "as though God were pleading through us" (2 Corinthians 5:20). Messengers must be:

Approved: divine approval – their acceptability, what God thinks.

Entrusted: divine trust – their fidelity. This shows what God does through those who are faithful to His Name and Word. One aspect of this applies to what we could call "priestly preaching." 1 Peter 2:9 calls for those who know Christ as Priest to "show forth the excellencies of Him who called you out of darkness into His marvellous light" (RV), but does this give us the liberty to share our royal priesthood witness with other believers? If so, they would have similar freedom to share in the holy priesthood's worship in verse 5; but, since verse 5 doesn't permit an open table, verse 9 doesn't permit an open platform. In Acts 2:41, response to the gospel is like the first lamp of the lampstand, which shows how dependent the testimony of the house of God is on the gospel of God. As armies need recruitment, as schools need new enrolment, so also churches of God need to win souls otherwise they will die.

Tested: divine pleasure – their authority. When Jesus said, "I have given them Your word", was He referring to the Old Testament from Genesis to Malachi, or to the revelation of His will that should spearhead their service? He was giving marching orders to witnesses of a gospel that demands obligation as well as reconciliation and calling us to take His commission seriously by emphasising obedience in our preaching. The kind of gospel we preach will determine the kind of disciples we make. Diluting the message always leads to deceiving the sinner and demeaning the Saviour. Another danger lies in encouraging the unsaved to worship before they have yielded to Christ's ownership and discipleship.

What an honour to bring sinners to the blood of Jesus: to 1) its shedding, and 2) its sprinkling.

1. Cleansing the sinner 2. Claiming the saint
Acceptance Obedience
Atonement Government
Union Communion
Redemption Obligation

In days when Christ is blasphemed, His name taken in vain, when it's politically correct to ridicule Christianity whilst fearing to offend Islam, etc., our world needs to hear a gospel that exalts the Saviour and excites the sinner. In darkening days our world needs to hear a brighter gospel, and the anticipation of our Saviour's return urges us to be among those who give it its proper place. We should preach as we have never preached before, reach as we have never reached before, and shine as we have never shone before, so that many will get a glimpse of His glory through the preacher and the preaching before the church goes home at the rapture and the light of the world goes out. In some way, we have to take the message down to the people, but our highest honour is in bringing the people up to the message. Let's lift them up "in power, in the Holy Spirit, and in much assurance."

Each new height reveals another far outshining every other,
And farther heights to conquer when it's gained
On to higher peaks and pleasant,
Not content with just the present,
Ever upward and to heights not yet attained.

The Use of the Word 'Church' in Ephesians

"And He put all things in subjection under His feet, and gave Him as head over all things to the church, which is His body, the fullness of Him who fills all in all" (Ephesians 1:22-23).

"There is one body and one Spirit ..." (Ephesians 4:4).

"... that He might present to Himself the church in all her glory, having no spot or wrinkle or any such thing; but that she would be holy and blameless" (Ephesians 5:27).

* * *

As we have seen, the overall theme of this book has been a wonderful presentation of the church the body of Christ. The word "church" in Ephesians is found nine times and is the same word "*ekklēsia*". It is found over 112 times in the New Testament and has various uses such as the following:

1. An assembly of Christians gathered for worship in a religious meeting;
2. A company of Christian, or of those who, hoping for eternal salvation through Jesus Christ, observe their own religious rites, hold their own religious meetings, and manage their own affairs, according to regulations prescribed for the body for order's sake;
3. Those who anywhere, in a city, village, constitute such a company and are united into one body;

4. The whole body of Christians scattered throughout the earth;

5. The assembly of faithful Christians already dead and received into heaven.

(Source: the Blue Letter Bible - online)

The importance of context and terminology

So it would seem important to understand what the word church is describing by the context of the scripture containing the word. As we study the new testament, we find that the Spirit of God may use a slightly different word to make a distinction of what is being communicated or He may use the context of the narrative to insure an understanding of the meaning. Terminology is also used to help us understand and relate to the subject being presented and thus we have the terms in Ephesians 1, "feet, head, body." Here we are presented with the authority of Christ and His relationship with those who He has purchased with his blood. All things will be subjected to Him and we see this described as 'under His feet.' Then we are given a view of His relationship with believers as he is given to them, His church, as Head. There is to be no doubt as to who is over all things, it is Christ and He is seen in His authority as the one who is the Head.

Some might suggest that Jesus Christ is the 'head' of the body in a literal way. Again we find illustrative context to help us understand what is being presented to us in terms of the body. 1 Corinthians 12:15-20 gives us a clear understanding:

"For the body is not one member, but many. If the foot says, "Because I am not a hand, I am not a part of the body," it is not for this reason any the less a part of the body.And if the ear says, "Because I am not an eye, I am not a part of the body." it is not for this reason any the less a part of the body. If the whole body were an eye, where would the hearing be? If the whole were hearing, where would the sense of smell be? But now God has placed the members, each one of them, in the body, just as He desired. If they were all one member, where would the body be? But now there are many members, but one body."

So we are all members of the body and we all need each other as we acknowledge the authority of the one who is 'over us all', the Head, Christ Jesus.

An expression of the Church the Body, a local Church of disciples

Again it is important to understand the use of the word church in its context. There are two dominate uses of the word 'church' in the new testament. The first we have been discussing in our study of Ephesians, that being the church which is His body. This is made up of all believers, those that are in Christ; past, present and future. The other use of the term church is for the local gathered together believers that formed a Church of God. This is seen in the singular and is also used in the plural as 'Churches of God.'

When looking at the word church "ekklēsia," it is mentioned over 112 times, including 14 times speaking of the body of Christ, 97 times as local gatherings of disciples in various cities and towns; and 1 time as the "firstborn who are registered in heaven" (Hebrews 12:23). Of the 97 local references, 57 speak of a single local church and 40 the aggregate of local churches. What is exciting to understand is that the rich characteristics of the Body teaching are to be seen expressed out in living terms within the local church.When we take into consideration the extent of the references to the 'Church of God' such as at Corinth; "To the Church of God which is at Corinth …" (1 Corinthians 1:2) we come to the conclusion that local churches are to reflect the ownership of God and therefore demonstrate the excellencies of Him who has called us out of darkness into His marvelous light.

Paul was a church planter and as he communicated to the saints in a given location he would address them in various ways. We have seen his address in both letters to the believers in Corinth as the 'Church of God in Corinth.' We see in Philippians that he addresses the saints in Philippi, including the overseers and deacons, and in Galatians he addresses several local churches as 'to the churches of Galatia.' He says to the Galatians that in his former life he persecuted the 'Church of God' and tried to destroy it. So it seems logical that the local church was called a Church of God and was known and identified as saints in a specific location.

We should never forget that this study is not about a 'title' but rather the living out of God's Word, "to walk in a manner worthy of the calling with which you have been called, with all humility and gentleness, with patience, showing tolerance for one another in love, being diligent to preserve the unity of the Spirit in the bond of peace" (Ephesians 4:1-3).

There were other names used to describe or emphasize particular aspects of these local churches:

- The church in a house (Romans 16:5);
- the church of the living God (1 Timothy 3:15);
- the church throughout all Judea, Galilee and Samaria (Acts 9:31);
- the churches of the saints (1 Corinthians 14:33); and
- the churches of Christ (Romans 16:16).

So it varied as to where they were gathered, how far and wide they were linked to each other, and the character and authority of the church. The names reflect the local church makeup; their authority 'of God', their composition 'of Saints', and character 'of Christ'

A matrix of comparison thoughts has been produced for study material and should be helpful in understanding that the term "the Church of God" is not the same as the term "the Church the body."

The Church the Body of Christ	The Church or Churches of God
1. There is one body Ephesians 4:4, Romans 12:4-5	There are many churches of God 1 Thessalonians 2:14, 2 Thessalonians 1:1-4
2. Comprised of all believers Galatians 3:28	Believers in the Lord Jesus gathered locally 1 Corinthians 1:2 and link Acts 18:8
3. Made up of those who believe in Christ Matthew 16:18	Made up of disciples who obey the Lord and follow His direction Acts 2:41; Romans 6:17
4. Entered by baptism in the Spirit 1 Corinthians 12:13	Baptism in water and added to other disciples Acts 2:41; Acts 18:8-11
5. Depends on initial God's will and doing 1 Corinthians 1:30	Requires continuance in God's word and obedience Revelation 2:5
6. Cannot be put away from the Body John 6:37; John 10:28, Ephesians 5:27	Can be put away because of sin 1 Corinthians 5:13 Wrongfully put away by man 3 John 10
7. Cannot wander away from John 18:9; 1 Corinthians 6:19	May drift away and withdraw from 1 John 2:19
8. Christ Himself is the builder Matthew 16:18	Men build the local Church of God 1 Corinthians 3:9-10
9. Cannot be destroyed! Matthew 16:18	Can be made havoc of... Galatians 1:13
10. No distinction between male and female Galatians 3:28	Distinction between male and female 1 Corinthians 14:34; 11:5
11. Nourished by Christ Ephesians 5:29	Cared for by elders Acts 20:28; Hebrews 13:17
12. A truth hidden in the Old Testament Ephesians 3:3-5	A truth revealed in the Old Testament Exodus 25:8; I Kings 8:27 (In principle or pattern)

Prayer in Ephesians

"For this reason I too, having heard of the faith in the Lord Jesus which exists among you and your love for all the saints, do not cease giving thanks for you , while making mention of you in my prayers ..." (Ephesians 1: 15-16)

"For this reason I kneel before the Father, from whom every family in heaven and on earth derives its name. I pray that out of his glorious riches he may strengthen you with power through his Spirit in your inner being, so that Christ may dwell in your hearts through faith. And I pray that you, being rooted and established in love, may have power, together with all the Lord's holy people, to grasp how wide and long and high and deep is the love of Christ, and to know this love that surpasses knowledge—that you may be filled to the measure of all the fullness of God. (Ephesians 3:14-19 NIV)

* * *

We see in our study of Ephesians the deep desire that Paul had for the Church in Ephesus and it is revealed in his prayers. That should be a key insight as to what we pray for but we are also challenged as to how to pray. Our Lord Jesus shares some tremendous insight regarding how to pray to God in Matthew 6:5-13.

"And now about prayer. When you pray, don't be like the hypocrites who love to pray publicly on street corners and in the synagogues where everyone can see them. I assure you, that is all the reward they will ever get. But when you pray, go away by yourself, shut the door behind you, and pray to your Father secretly. Then your Father, who knows all secrets, will reward you.

"When you pray, don't babble on and on as people of other religions do. They think prayers are answered only by repeating words over and over again. Don't be like them, because your Father knows exactly what you need even before you ask him! Pray like this: Our Father in heaven, may your Name be honored. May Your Kingdom come soon. May Your will be done here on earth, just as it is in heaven. Give us our food for today, and forgive us our sins, just as we have forgiven those who have sinned against us. And don't let us yield to temptation, but deliver us from the evil one." (From the New Living Translation)

In the above verses, Jesus shares ...

How not to pray

- Verse 5: We are to pray in secret, not the way people did in His day — praying out loud publicly, primarily to just be seen and heard.
- Verse 6: Jesus asks us to go to a private place since our Heavenly Father already knows what we are going to pray about.
- Verse 7: Jesus tells us not to ramble on and on, as people of other religions do, or be repetitious with our words. God, our heavenly Father, would have us be specific about our prayer.
- Verse 8: Jesus reiterates that the believer is not to pray repetitiously like the heathen.

Next, Jesus, teaches us ...

How to pray

- Verse 9: Jesus says we should give honor to God and His name.
- Verse 10: We are to pray for His Kingdom to come, and for His will to be done, that there would be a heavenly or godly presence here on earth.
- Verse 11: We are to pray for daily provision.
- Verse 12: We are to pray and ask for forgiveness for our sins, and for others who have wronged us.
- Verse 13: We are to pray and ask God to keep us from being tempted, and to deliver us from Satan and his power.

Other New Testament writers describe other ways to pray. Paul, in Philippians 4:6, says that we should pray for everything with thanksgiving. Paul, who wrote several books of the New Testament, often began and ended his letters in prayer for the saints. We have seen his prayer desire for the Saints in Ephesus in this study. Specifically, Paul prays for God's grace, peace, love, and faith among believers.

Peter, in 1 Peter 5:7, exhorts us to cast all our care upon God, because He cares about us. In verse 8, Peter warns us that Satan seeks to devour the believer. James 1:5 says we can pray and ask God for wisdom, but this should be done in faith. James 4:1-4 says that when we pray, we often pray or ask out of our own selfish ambition. James 4:15 exhorts that we need to pray for God's will to be done in our lives.

In the Old Testament, Moses prayed to God almost constantly on behalf of the Israelites — for God's mercy and graciousness in dealing with their sins. Abraham prayed persistently for his relative Lot, who lived in Sodom, that God would spare Him. You will recall the 'prayer of Jabez' in 1 Chronicles 4: 9-10; "Oh that You would bless me indeed and enlarge my border, and that Your hand might be with me, and that You would keep me from harm that it may not pain me!" David often spoke to God and he prayed for the peace of Jerusalem in Psalm 122:6.

The protocol on how to pray covers several ways of prayer. The primary focus of prayer is the intent. Does the prayer honor God and exalt His name? What is the purpose behind the prayer? Is it personal gain or ambition? Do you pray for others to be blessed and encouraged? Are your prayers done in secret and in humility? Are your prayers focused on obtaining godly wisdom, counsel, and direction? God is pleased with these prayers and answers them.

How often are we to pray?

The Bible says pray without ceasing (1 Thessalonians 5:17). This is what Paul was doing for the Ephesians as he did not cease to give thanks for them and mentioned them in his prayers (Ephesians 1:16).

What should we pray for? What if we do not know how to pray? The Bible says the Holy Spirit will help us pray (Romans 8:26-27).

How do we pray to God?

Prayer is essentially putting your request, concern, or issue before the Lord, and trusting Him to answer them. Matthew 18:3 says we need to pray with the heart of little children, simple, reverent, specific, and trusting.

To whom do we pray?

Before we can answer, "why should we pray," we must know to whom we pray. This is a challenge and can be helpful as we spend time in prayer. It is easy for us to just want to quickly say a few words and feel good about it. But we must remember 'Who' we speak to. Having this awareness can set the tone for what we are about to say and how we think about our time of prayer. There is only one supreme Creator and Sovereign God. There is only one way to Him and that is through His only Son, Jesus Christ. God, our Heavenly Father, is the only one we can be assured of who hears and answers our prayers and He is the God of amazing love, mercy, and forgiveness:

- By Him, all things are possible. Jesus says in Mark 10:27, "Humanly speaking, it is impossible. But not with God. Everything is possible with God."
- "We do not ask because we deserve help, but because you are so merciful." (Daniel 9:18) (Mercy means showing favor, compassion, and kindness.)
- God's ultimate demonstration of love is forgiveness of the sins each of us have committed. "For God so loved the world that he gave his only Son, so that everyone who believes in him will not perish but have eternal life. God did not send his Son into the world to condemn it, but to save it" (John 3:16-17).
- "If we confess our sins, He is faithful and righteous to forgive us our sins and to cleanse us from all unrighteousness. (1 John 1:9)

He is the only true God who has done this, and is the only true God able to do so. But His enemy, Satan, has sent many false gods to deceive mankind. Do not be deceived nor allow anything or anyone to take priority over the only true and living God.

For what should we pray?

Prayer is the key to the heart of God. Prayer is the only way to a real and personal relationship with God. So what we pray for is also just as important as how we pray. It's a challenge to contrast our prayer time with that of Paul's in Ephesians. Just as the prayer of the Lord in Matthew 6 gives guidance to how to pray, the Spirit directs us in Ephesians as to what we should be praying about:

- Spiritual wisdom and revelation in the knowledge of Him.

- That the eyes of our heart might be enlightened.
- That we might know what is the hope of His calling.
- That Christ may dwell in our hearts by faith.

There are other things that we might consider:

- Pray confessing our sins and accepting His forgiveness.
- Pray that His will be done in our lives, that His Holy Spirit guide us, and that we be filled with the fullness of Him.
- Thanksgiving for all the ways He blesses us.
- Pray when we are ill, lonely, going through trials or interceding for others (James 5:14-16, 2 Corinthians 12:9-10).

There is nothing we can't pray about. There are abundant references to prayer in the Bible so we have lots to guide us. The Bible tells us to "Pray without ceasing" and "in everything to give thanks to the Lord." When we choose to have a positive attitude, we realize we have received many blessings for which to give God praise.

We find intimacy with God through communicating with Him in prayer. We go to Him in faith, knowing that He hears and answers all our prayers Be confident that God knows and wants what is best for us; so ask that His will be done in all we seek from Him. Then, thank Him for it, even though it hasn't happened yet. We are reminded in Hebrews 4:14-16, that we have a high priest who knows and cares for us:

"Therefore, since we have a great high priest who has passed through the heavens, Jesus the Son of God, let us hold fast our confession. For we do not have a high priest who cannot sympathize with our weaknesses, but One who has been tempted in all things as we are, yet without sin. Therefore let us draw near with confidence to the throne of grace, so that we may receive mercy and find grace to help in time of need."

Above all, pray with sincerity, honor, and humility before the Almighty God. "The effective prayer of a righteous man can accomplish much" (James 5:16).

ABOUT THE PUBLISHER

Hayes Press (www.hayespress.org) is a registered charity in the United Kingdom, whose primary mission is to disseminate the Word of God, mainly through literature. It is one of the largest distributors of gospel tracts and leaflets in the United Kingdom, with over 100 titles and many thousands dispatched annually. In addition to paperbacks and eBooks, Hayes Press also publishes Plus Eagles' Wings, a fun and educational Bible magazine for children, and Golden Bells, a popular daily Bible reading calendar in wall or desk formats.

If you would like to contact Hayes Press, there are a number of ways you can do so:

• By mail: c/o The Barn, Flaxlands, Royal Wootton Bassett, Wiltshire, UK SN4 8DY

• By phone: 01793 850598

• By eMail: info@hayespress.org

• via Facebook: www.facebook.com/hayespress.org

MORE FROM TRAINING FOR SERVICE

TRANSFORMED BY THE GOSPEL - A BIBLE STUDY OF THE BOOK OF ROMANS

1. AN INTRODUCTION TO THE BOOK OF ROMANS
2. SENT AND SEPARATED (ROMANS 1:1-17)
3. GUILTY (ROMANS 1:18–3:20)
4. JUSTIFIED (ROMANS 3:21–5:21)
5. COMMITTED (ROMANS 6)
6. PERPLEXED (ROMANS 7)
7. VICTORIOUS (ROMANS 8)
8. SET ASIDE (ROMANS 9)
9. INGRAFTED (ROMANS 10 & 11)
10. GIFTED (ROMANS 12)
11. YIELDED (ROMANS 13)
12. LIBERATED (ROMANS 14)
13. FILLED (ROMANS 15)
14. UNITED (ROMANS 16)

SERVING GOD ACCEPTABLY - A BIBLE STUDY OF THE BOOK OF HEBREWS

www.ingramcontent.com/pod-product-compliance
Lightning Source LLC
Chambersburg PA
CBHW060115050426

42448CB00010B/1876